interchange

English for international communication

Jack C. Richards

with Jonathan Hull
and Susan Proctor

2

Student's Book

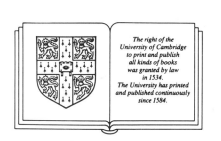

The right of the
University of Cambridge
to print and publish
all kinds of books
was granted by law
in 1534.
The University has printed
and published continuously
since 1584.

Cambridge University Press

Cambridge • New York • Port Chester • Melbourne • Sydney

Published by the Press Syndicate of the University of Cambridge
The Pitt Building, Trumpington Street, Cambridge CB2 1RP
40 West 20th Street, New York, NY 10011, USA
10 Stamford Road, Oakleigh, Melbourne 3166, Australia

© Cambridge University Press 1991

First published 1991
Second printing 1991

Printed in the United States of America

Library of Congress Cataloging-in-Publication Data
Richards, Jack C.
Interchange : English for international communication : student's
book 2 / Jack C. Richards with Jonathan Hull and Susan Proctor.
p.   cm.
ISBN 0-521-37681-5
1. English language – Textbooks for foreign speakers.
2. Communication, International.   I. Hull, Jonathan.   II. Proctor,
Susan.   III. Title.
PE1128.R4572   1991
428.2′4 – dc20   90-1912
                                                      CIP

British Library Cataloguing in Publication Data
Richards, Jack C.
Interchange : English for international communication.
Student's bk. 2.
1. English language.   Usage
I. Title   II. Hull, Jonathan   III. Proctor, Susan
428
ISBN 0-521-37681-5

ISBN 0 521 37681 5 Student's Book Two
ISBN 0 521 37682 3 Teacher's Manual Two
ISBN 0 521 37683 1 Workbook Two
ISBN 0 521 37534 7 Class Cassette Set Two
ISBN 0 521 37535 5 Student Cassette Two

Book design: Peter Ducker
Layouts: Circa 86, Inc.
Cover design: Tom Wharton

Illustrators:
Jack and Judith De Graffenried
Mark Kaufman
Bill Thomson
Sam Viviano
Kam Yu/Reno Art Works

Contents

Plan of Book 2

	Topics	Functions	Grammar/Pronunciation
UNIT 1	**Topics** People; education; childhood; the past	**Functions** Talking about oneself; introducing oneself; talking about someone else	**Grammar** Past tense for narration; past tense and *used to* for habitual actions **Pronunciation** Reductions with *were* and *did*
UNIT 2	**Topics** Cities; locations; directions; buildings	**Functions** Talking about a city; giving directions	**Grammar** Indirect questions; sequence markers; imperatives **Pronunciation** Question intonation
UNIT 3	**Topics** Housing; prices; cities	**Functions** Describing homes, neighborhoods, cities; describing positive and negative features; making comparisons	**Grammar** Adverbs and adjectives; comparisons using adjectives **Pronunciation** Sentence stress

Review of Units 1–3

	Topics	Functions	Grammar/Pronunciation
UNIT 4	**Topics** Food; experiences; instructions; recipes	**Functions** Describing experiences; giving instructions	**Grammar** Past tense and present perfect; two-part verbs **Pronunciation** Word stress
UNIT 5	**Topics** Travel; vacations; plans	**Functions** Giving advice; describing things to do in a city; describing plans	**Grammar** Modal verbs; future with present continuous and *going to* **Pronunciation** Reduced form of *going to*
UNIT 6	**Topics** Requests; complaints; apologies	**Functions** Making requests; accepting/refusing requests; complaining; apologizing; giving excuses	**Grammar** Imperatives; requests with modals **Pronunciation** Reductions with *could* and *would*

Review of Units 4–6

	Topics	Functions	Grammar/Pronunciation
UNIT 7	**Topics** Gadgets; machines; appliances	**Functions** Describing what things are for; describing problems with things; suggesting causes for problems	**Grammar** Infinitives; gerunds; countable and uncountable nouns **Pronunciation** Stress in compound nouns
UNIT 8	**Topics** Holidays; festivals; customs	**Functions** Describing holidays, festivals, customs, and special events	**Grammar** Relative clauses of time; adverbial clauses of time **Pronunciation** Sentence stress and rhythm

Listening	Writing/Reading	Interchange Activity	
Listening Listening for references to past, present, and future; listening to complaints and possible solutions	**Writing** Writing about hopes for the future **Reading** Opinion poll about the past, present, and future; unusual laws	**Interchange** Finding out people's opinions	UNIT **9**

Listening Listening to statements and choosing a correct response; listening for positive or negative opinions	**Writing** Writing about the family **Reading** Facts about the world of work; what handwriting tells about personality	**Interchange** Describing work, skills, and abilities	UNIT **10**
Listening Listening for specific facts about landmarks and a country	**Writing** Writing about a country **Reading** Famous landmarks; Brazil	**Interchange** Culture quiz	UNIT **11**
Listening Listening for references to the past and present; listening about a person's life	**Writing** Writing a biography **Reading** Some facts about celebrities; story of a refugee	**Interchange** Conducting an interview	UNIT **12**

Listening Listening to descriptions of books and movies	**Writing** Writing a movie review **Reading** The top ten movies; movie reviews	**Interchange** Movie quiz	UNIT **13**
Listening Listening for excuses; listening for telephone messages	**Writing** Writing telephone messages **Reading** Languages; the truth about lying	**Interchange** Finding out about likes, dislikes, and wishes	UNIT **14**
Listening Listening to advice and suggestions	**Writing** Writing to an advice columnist **Reading** Fortunes; newspaper advice column	**Interchange** Talking about predicaments	UNIT **15**

Acknowledgments

Illustrators

Jack and Judith DeGraffenried 33, 46 *(top)*, 49 *(bottom)*, 88, 96

Mark Kaufman 12, 25, 36 *(bottom)*, 38, 43 *(all)*, 46 *(bottom)*, 90

Bill Thomson 2, 4, 10, 24, 26 *(bottom)*, 29 *(top)*, 31, 34, 37, 41, 49 *(top)*, 51, 57, 62, 63, 65 *(bottom)*, 69, 71, 74, 80 *(bottom)*, 81, 84, 95, 97, 114

Sam Viviano 9, 14, 22, 23, 27, 29 *(bottom)*, 30, 35, 36 *(top)*, 40, 45 *(both)*, 53, 54, 56, 58, 61, 65 *(top)*, 76, 77, 80 *(top)*, 86, 91, 93, 94, 102, 109, 110

Kam Yu/Reno Art Works 19, 26 *(top)*

Photographic Credits

The authors and publishers are grateful for permission to reproduce the following photographs.

2 Fredric Petters

3 *(both)* © H. Scott Heist 1990 for Lehigh University

4 Fredric Petters

5 *Stand By Me*

6 *(clockwise from top)* Benn Mitchell/The Image Bank; © 1989 Alvis Upitis/The Image Bank; © The Stock Market/ Gabe Palmer 1988

7 *(top to bottom)* Steve Schapiro/Gamma Liaison; The Bettmann Archive; SuperStock, Inc.; UPI/Bettmann Newsphotos

10 *(clockwise from top left)* New York Convention and Visitors Bureau; © Rudi Von Briel, New York; Pamela J. Zilly/The Image Bank

13 *(top)* San Francisco Convention and Visitors Bureau, photo by Kerrick James; *(bottom)* © Don Klein, San Francisco

15 *(left to right)* George Hunter/H. Armstrong Roberts; Van D. Bucher/Photo Researchers; R. Krubner/H. Armstrong Roberts

17 *(left)* Tourism Authority of Thailand; *(right)* Japan National Tourist Organization

18 Courtesy of Café de la Paix, Paris

20 *(lower left both)* FPG International; *(right)* H. Armstrong Roberts

21 *(left)* Paolo Koch/Photo Researchers; *(right)* Guillaume de Laubier/Gamma

26 Courtesy of Ally & Gargano

30 *(top)* New York Convention and Visitors Bureau; *(bottom)* *The Bride of Frankenstein*

32 Fredric Petters

34 *(all)* Fredric Petters

41 Courtesy of Club Med

42 Fredric Petters

44 *(left to right)* Copyright © The Sharper Image; Sony Walkman® Personal Stereo with Mega Bass®; courtesy of Hammacher Schlemmer, 1-800-543-3366; courtesy of Radio Shack, A Division of Tandy Corporation

47 *(clockwise from top right)* B.N. Genius®/The Sporting Edge® Companies, 1-800-468-4410; courtesy of Rabbit Systems, Inc.; source unknown; courtesy of Radio Shack, A Division of Tandy Corporation; B.N. Genius®/The Sporting Edge® Companies

50 *(ex. 5 left)* SuperStock, Inc.; *(ex. 5 right)* © Bill Lyons, Amman, Jordan; *(ex. 6, clockwise)* Hong Kong Tourist Association; © 1980 Syndey Byrd; John Bryson/The Image Bank; *(ex. 7)* © Theodore Anderson

51 Lou Jones/The Image Bank

52 *(top to bottom)* Alain Evrand/Photo Researchers; Sabine Weiss/Photo Researchers; © The Stock Market/Ted Horowitz

55 *(left to right)* National Air and Space Museum Smithsonian Institution Photo No. A-2574; courtesy of Air France; National Aeronautics and Space Administration

56 H. Armstrong Roberts

58 Mark Boulton/Photo Researchers

59 *(left)* Fredric Petters; *(right)* Vidocq

60 Courtesy of Panasonic

61 © Jacques Lowe 1990

64 *(clockwise from top left)* Courtesy of International Business Machines Corporation; © H. Scott Heist 1990 for Lehigh University; © copyright Rich Cox; SuperStock, Inc.

66 *(clockwise from top right)* Carol Friedman/courtesy of CBS Masterworks; Harry Langdon/Gamma Liaison; Georges de Keerle/Gamma Liaison

68 Courtesy of Panama Canal Commission

70 *(left)* Susan McCartney/Photo Researchers; *(middle and right)* Washington Convention and Visitors Association

72 *(all)* Guatemala Tourist Commission

73 *(top)* Nilo Lima/Photo Researchers; *(others)* © Don Klein, San Francisco

75 SuperStock, Inc.

76 *(left)* Theo Westenberger/Sygma; *(right)* Tom Zimberoff/ Sygma

78 *(left to right)* Edinger/Gamma Liaison; The Kobal Collection/SuperStock, Inc.; AP/Wide World Photos

79 *(top)* Reuters/Bettmann Newsphotos; *(bottom)* courtesy of Regina Wilson

81 *(left)* Susan McCartney/Photo Researchers; *(right)* H. Armstrong Roberts

82 *Rebel Without a Cause*

83 David R. Frazier/Photo Researchers

85 *(top) The Shining; (bottom clockwise from top left)* United Artists/SuperStock, Inc.; Museum of Modern Art, Film Stills Archive; *2001;* The Kobal Collection/ SuperStock, Inc.

86 Copyright © BBC

87 G. Rancinan/Sygma

88 *10 Minutes a Day* language series, courtesy of Sunset Books, Lane Publishing Co., Menlo Park, CA

98 Fredric Petters

101 *(clockwise from top)* Lo Linkert; courtesy of *Private Eye;* Wayne Stayskal

107 *(left)* Washington Convention and Visitors Association; *(right)* McKinney/Photo Researchers

108 *(upper right, from top to bottom)* Shostal Associates/ SuperStock, Inc.; © Sam Saylor; © The Stock Market/J. Messerschmidt 1987; *(bottom, clockwise from left)* Greater Boston Convention and Visitors Bureau; New York Convention and Visitors Bureau

111 *(video camera, telephone, television)* Courtesy of D.C.A. Inc.; *(mixer, flashlight, iron)* Courtesy of Black & Decker; *(fax machine)* Courtesy of Radio Shack, A Division of Tandy Corporation

112 *(video camera, microwave oven)* Courtesy of D.C.A. Inc.; *(toaster, coffeemaker, can opener)* Courtesy of Black & Decker; *(personal stereo, answering machine)* Courtesy of Radio Shack, A Division of Tandy Corporation

113 *(clockwise from top right)* Inger Abrahmsen/Photo Researchers; © The Stock Market/Gabe Palmer 1989; Elyse Lewin/The Image Bank; Four by Five

116 *(clockwise from top right)* MGM/SuperStock, Inc.; The Bettmann Archive; Mark Sennett/Gamma; *Camille;* SuperStock, Inc.

117 George Rose/Gamma Liaison

118 *(clockwise from top right)* Bennett-Spooner/Gamma; Lucas Films/SuperStock; © Shooting Star; © Shooting Star; Quinn/Gamma

119 Joe Traver/Gamma Liaison

120 *Jaws; King Kong; (top right)* Gamma Liaison; *Dracula*

Authors' Acknowledgments

A great number of people assisted us in writing **Interchange.** We owe particular thanks to the following:

Our **reviewers,** who gave helpful comments on preliminary versions of the course:

Jeffrey Bright, Steven Brown, Suzanne Robertshaw, Chuck Sandy, Mark Sawyer, Barbara Strodt-Lopez, and Rita Wong.

The **students** and **teachers** in the following schools and institutes where the course was pilot tested:

Alianza Cultural Uruguay-Estados Unidos de America, Montevideo, Uruguay; **American Language Program, American Center,** Paris, France; **Associação Alumni,** São Paulo, Brazil; **Centre de Récherches et d'Applications Pedagogiques en Langues,** Nancy, France; **D. B. Hood Community School,** Toronto, Ontario, Canada; **Eurocentres,** Alexandria, Virginia, U.S.A.; **Instituto Cultural Mexicano-Norteamericano de Jalisco,** Guadalajara, Mexico; **Intensive English Program, University of Central Florida,** Orlando, Florida, U.S.A.; **Interac,** Tokyo, Japan; **Kanda Gaigo Gakuin,** Tokyo, Japan; **Loma Vista Adult Center, Mt. Diablo Adult Education,** Concord, California, U.S.A.; **Migros-Klub-Schule,** Bern, Switzerland; **Mohawk College, English Language Studies,** Hamilton, Ontario, Canada; **Ontario Welcome House,** Toronto, Ontario, Canada; **Panterra American School,** Fontanelle, Italy; **Sheridan College,** Mississauga, Ontario, Canada; **University of Pittsburgh English Language Institute,** Tokyo, Japan.

And our **editors** and **advisors** at Cambridge University Press, who guided us through the complex process of writing classroom materials:

Suzette André, Peter Donovan, Adrian du Plessis, Sandra Graham, Bob Greiner, Joan Gregory, Colin Hayes, Steven Maginn, Ellen Shaw, and Marjan van Schaik.

Introduction

Interchange is a three-level course in English as a second or foreign language for young adults and adults. The course covers the skills of listening, speaking, reading, and writing, with particular emphasis on listening and speaking. The primary goal of the course is to teach communicative competence – that is, the ability to communicate in English according to the situation, purpose, and roles of the participants. The language used in *Interchange* is American English; however, *Interchange* reflects the fact that English is the world's major language of international communication and is not limited to any one country, region, or culture. Level Two takes students from low intermediate to intermediate level.

Level Two builds on and extends the foundations for accurate and fluent communication established in Level One. Following a similar approach and methodology, Level Two extends grammatical, lexical, and functional skills, enabling learners to take part in genuine communication through the use of a wide variety of stimulating and challenging activities. The syllabus covered in Level Two incorporates review of key language features taught in Level One, allowing Level Two to be used in situations where students have not studied Level One.

COURSE LENGTH

Interchange is a self-contained course covering all four language skills. Each level covers between 60 and 90 hours of class instruction time. Depending on how the book is used, however, more or less time may be utilized. The Teacher's Manual gives detailed suggestions for optional activities to extend each unit. Where less time is available, the course can be taught in approximately 60 hours by reducing the amount of time spent on Interchange Activities, reading, writing, optional activities, and the Workbook.

COURSE COMPONENTS

Student's Book The Student's Book contains fifteen units, with a review unit after every three units. There are five review units in all. Following Unit 15 is a set of communication activities called Interchange Activities, one for each unit of the book. Unit Summaries, at the end of the Student's Book, contain lists of the key vocabulary and expressions used in each unit as well as grammar summaries.

Teacher's Manual A separate Teacher's Manual contains detailed suggestions on how to teach the course, lesson-by-lesson notes, an extensive set of optional follow-up activities, complete answer keys to the Student's Book and Workbook exercises, tests for use in class and test answer keys, and transcripts of those listening activities not printed in the Student's Book and in the five tests. The tests can be photocopied and distributed to students after each review unit is completed.

Workbook The Workbook contains stimulating and varied exercises that provide additional practice on the teaching points presented in the Student's Book. A variety of exercise types is used to develop students' skills in grammar, reading, writing, spelling, vocabulary, and pronunciation. The Workbook can be used both for classwork and for homework.

Class Cassettes A set of two cassettes for class use accompanies the Student's Book. The cassettes contain recordings of the conversations, grammar focus summaries, pronunciation exercises, and listening activities, as well as recordings of the listening exercises used in the tests. A variety of native-speaker voices and accents is used, as well as some nonnative speakers of English. Exercises that are recorded on the cassettes are indicated with the symbol ▭.

Student Cassette A cassette is also available for students to use for self-study. The Student Cassette contains selected recordings of conversations, grammar, and pronunciation exercises from the Student's Book.

APPROACH AND METHODOLOGY

Interchange teaches students to use English for everyday situations and purposes related to work, school, social life, and leisure. The underlying philosophy of the course is that learning a second language is more rewarding, meaningful, and effective when the language is used for authentic communication. Information-sharing activities provide a maximum amount of student-generated communication. Throughout *Interchange,* students have the opportunity to personalize the language they learn and make use of their own life experiences and world knowledge.

The course has the following key features:

Integrated Syllabus *Interchange* has an integrated, multi-skills syllabus that links grammar and communicative functions. The course recognizes grammar as an essential component of second language proficiency. However, it presents grammar communicatively, with controlled accuracy-based activities leading to fluency-based communicative practice. The syllabus also contains the four skills of listening, speaking, reading, and writing, as well as pronunciation and vocabulary.

Adult and International Content *Interchange* deals with contemporary topics that are of high interest and relevance to both students and teachers. Each unit includes real-world information on a variety of topics.

Enjoyable and Useful Learning Activities A wide variety of interesting and enjoyable activities forms the basis for each unit. The course makes extensive use of pair work, small group activities, role plays, and information-sharing activities. Practice exercises allow for a maximum amount of individual student practice and enable learners to personalize and apply the language they learn. Throughout the course, natural and useful language is presented that can be used in real-life situations.

WHAT EACH UNIT CONTAINS

Each unit in *Interchange* contains the following kinds of exercises:

Snapshot The Snapshots contain interesting information about the world, introduce the topic of the unit or part of the unit, and also develop vocabulary. Either the teacher can present these exercises in class as reading or discussion activities, or students can read them by themselves in class or for homework, using their dictionaries if necessary.

Conversation The Conversations introduce the new grammar of each unit in a communicative context and also present functions and conversational expressions. The teacher can either present the conversations with the Class Cassettes or read the dialogs aloud.

Pronunciation These exercises focus on important features of spoken English, including stress, rhythm, intonation, reductions, and sound contrasts.

Grammar Focus The new grammar of each unit is presented in color panels and is followed by practice activities that move from controlled to freer practice. These activities always give students a chance to use the grammar they have learned for real communication.

Listening The listening activities develop a wide variety of listening skills, including listening for gist, listening for details, and inferring meaning from context. These exercises often require completing an authentic task while listening, such as taking telephone messages. The recordings on the Class Cassettes contain both scripted and unscripted conversations with natural pauses, hesitations, and interruptions that occur in real speech.

Word Power The Word Power activities develop students' vocabulary through a variety of interesting tasks, such as word maps.

Writing The writing exercises include practical writing tasks that extend and reinforce the teaching points in the unit and help develop students' composition skills. The Teacher's Manual shows how to use these exercises to focus on the process of writing.

Reading The reading passages develop a variety of reading skills, including guessing words from context, skimming, scanning, and making inferences. Various text types adapted from authentic sources are used.

Interchange Activities The Interchange Activities are pair work and group work tasks, information-sharing tasks, and role plays that encourage real communication. These exercises are a central part of the course and allow students to extend and personalize what they have learned in each unit.

From the Authors

We hope that you will like using *Interchange* and find it useful, interesting, and fun. Our goal has been to provide teachers and students with activities that make the English class a time to look forward to and, at the same time, provide students with the skills they need to use English outside the classroom. Please let us know how you enjoyed it, and good luck!

Jack C. Richards
Jonathan Hull
Susan Proctor

1 A time to remember

1 GREETINGS AND INTRODUCTIONS 📼

1 Listen.

A: Hi. Can I give you a hand?
B: Oh, thanks.
A: By the way, I'm Maria. I'm in Apartment 203.
B: Oh? I'm moving into 204. My name is Noriko.
A: Nice to meet you.
B: Good to meet you, too.
A: And where are you from, Noriko?
B: I'm from Japan, from Osaka.
A: Oh, really? And are you going to school here?
B: No, I'm a reporter. I just started working for *World News.* And how about you, Maria? What do you do?
A: I'm a law student. I go to UC Berkeley. Say, why don't you come over for coffee later?
B: Oh, thanks. I'd love to.

2 *Pair work* Practice the conversation using your own information.

3 *Class activity* Now introduce yourself to some of your classmates. Then introduce two people you met to others in the class.

Useful expressions

Good morning/afternoon/evening.   What should I call you in class?
Hi! We haven't met. I'm . . .   Please call me . . .
What's your (first/last) name?   I'd like you to meet Mrs./Ms./Mr. . . .

2 TEACHER'S TURN

Ask your teacher these questions. Then think of three more questions and ask them.

Where are you from?   What languages do you speak?
Where did you go to school?   Where do you live?
What did you major in?   What should I call you in class?

3 GRAMMAR FOCUS: Past tense 📼

Where **were** you born?
I **was** born in Uruguay.

Were you born in the United States?
No, I **was** born in Chile.

Where **did** Ms. Hall **grow up**?
She **grew up** in Vancouver.

Did Peter **go** to school in Canada?
Yes, he **did.**

When **did** you **finish** school?
I **finished** school in 1990.

Did you **major** in English?
No, I **majored** in French.

1 Complete these conversations. Then compare with a partner and practice them.

A: Could you tell me a little about yourself? Where
.... grow up?
B: Well, I grew up in Ontario, Canada.
A: Oh? Did .... to college in
Toronto?
B: No, I .... I ....
college in Ottawa.

A: Where .... you .... to high school?
B: I .... to high school in San Diego,
California.
A: And .... you .... French in college?
B: No, I didn't. I studied Spanish and Portuguese.

A: Where .... you born?
B: I .... born in Madrid.

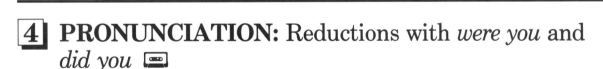

2 Now write five questions to ask your classmates. Use the past tense.

4 PRONUNCIATION: Reductions with *were you* and *did you* 📼

1 Listen to the reductions in these questions.

Where **were you** born? Where **did you** grow up? **Did you** go to college?

2 Now listen and practice these questions.

Where were you born?
Where did you go to school?
Did you take English in primary school?
What did you study in high school?

Did you go to a university?
When were you there?
What did you major in?

3 *Group work* Now take turns asking the questions you wrote in
Exercise 3.2. Use the reduced forms.

5 GETTING TO KNOW YOU

1 *Pair work* Take turns interviewing each other.

A: Hi! My name's . . .
B: Hello. I'm . . . Nice to meet you.
A: Good to meet you, too. Could you tell
   me a little about yourself?
B: Sure. What do you want to know?
A: Well, where are you from?
B: . . .

Then ask questions like these and take notes.

> Did you grow up there?
> Where did you go to high school?
> Did you study any foreign languages?
> When did you graduate from high school?
> Did you go to college or did you get a job
>   after high school?

2 *Class activity* Now use your notes and introduce your partner to
the class. Start like this.

> I'd like to introduce Gabrielle. She's from Germany, and she grew up
> in a small town near Munich. . . .

6 LISTENING 📼

1 Listen to people talking about a famous singer.

2 Now listen again and complete these notes.
Then compare with a partner.

He is a famous singer. He was born in ....
in .... He had a serious ....
accident in 1963. He learned to sing and play the
guitar in the .... He .... his first
song contest in .... In 1970, his song
"Guendoline" became a hit in .... He
quickly became popular in Europe and in
.... He won the ....
Eurovision Song Contest. His records sold over
.... million copies by 1980. His most famous
song in .... is "To All the ....
I've Loved ...." with Willie Nelson.

3 Do you know this singer's name? (Answer on page 134.)

4

7 WORD POWER: Verbs

1 *Pair work* Match verbs in list A with opposites in list B.

A

a) ask   f) send
b) give   g) sell
c) go   h) sit
d) love   i) start
e) remember   j) win

B

.... answer   .... hate
.... buy   .... receive
.... come   .... lose
.... finish   .... stand
.... forget   .... take

2 Now write down the past tense forms of the verbs above. Compare with a partner. Then use six of the verbs in sentences.

When I was in high school I loved math, but I hated English.

8 SNAPSHOT

THE 80'S

1980	Ronald Reagan is elected President of the United States.
1981	Prince Charles of Britain marries Lady Diana Spencer.
1982	Italy wins the World Soccer Cup.
1983	Sally K. Ride becomes the first U.S. woman in space.
1984	George Orwell's book *1984* becomes the best-selling book in North America.
1985	Mikhail Gorbachev becomes leader of the USSR.
1986	Spain and Portugal join the European Community.
1987	Van Gogh's painting *Sunflowers* sells for $39.9 million.
1988	Australia celebrates its 200th birthday.
1989	East Germany opens the Berlin Wall.

Discussion

Can you think of three other important world events that happened in the eighties?

What is the most important thing that happened to you in the eighties?

9 CONVERSATION 📼

1 Listen.

Ann: I just saw a great video, *Stand By Me.*
Jeff: Oh, yeah. I loved that movie! It really reminded me of my childhood.
Claudio: Me, too! What's your favorite childhood memory, Jeff?
Jeff: Um, let me see. Oh, I remember . . . My best friend and I built a treehouse in the backyard. We used to play in it all summer. It was really fun!

2 Now listen to the rest of the conversation and take notes. What do Ann and Claudio say about their childhoods? What is their favorite memory?

10 GRAMMAR FOCUS: *Used to* 🔲

What games **did** you **use to** play as a child? I **used to** play ''Monopoly.''	**Did** you **use to** have a hobby? Yes, I **used to** collect stamps.

1 Complete these sentences. Then compare with a partner.

a) In primary school, I used to . . .
b) For our summer vacations, we used to . . .
c) I used to be . . . , but I'm not anymore.
d) After school, my best friend and I used to . . .

2 Now write five sentences about yourself using the past tense or **used to.** Then compare with a partner.

11 MEMORIES

1 *Pair work* Ask these questions and other questions of your own.

Where did you use to live as a child?
What's your favorite childhood memory?
Where did you go to school?
What sports did you play?
Where did you use to go on vacation?
Did you have a part-time job?

2 *Class activity* Tell the class two interesting things about your partner.

12 LISTENING 🔲

Listen and check the correct response.

a) .... No, I wasn't.
   .... Yes, I used to.

b) .... Yes, I was.
   .... No, I took French.

c) .... From 1986 to 1990.
   .... In Mexico City.

d) .... Yes, I played football.
   .... Yes, it is.

e) .... Yes, in a restaurant.
   .... No, I majored in economics.

f) .... Yes, we used to.
   .... No, not really.

▶ **Interchange 1:**
Class profile
Discover some interesting facts about your classmates! Turn to page 102.

13 WRITING

1 Write about the things you used to do as a child.

When I was 4 years old, my family moved to Oregon. We had an old 2-story house and a big yard to play in. My older brother and I used to play lots of games together. In the summer, my favorite outdoor game was "hide and seek." It was both fun and scary because we...

2 *Group work* Take turns reading your compositions aloud and answer any questions.

14 READING: Remembering the sixties

What do you know about the 1960s?
Do you know the names of any famous singers or pop groups?
How were fashions different then?

1 Read this passage and choose the best heading for each paragraph.

Paragraph 1

.... Youth Rules the World
.... The Youngest Millionaire

Paragraph 2

.... The Peace Movement
.... Changes in Fashion and the Arts

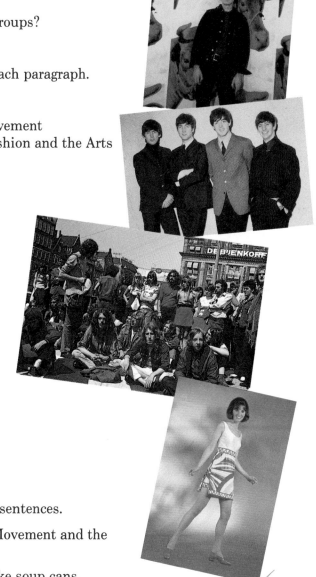

There are many things people remember about the sixties. Some people remember it for mini-skirts, the Beatles, hippies, and the flower children. It was a time when young people "owned" the world and thought that anything was possible. In art, fashion, and music, the big names were often in their early twenties, and some of them were already millionaires! The sixties was a time when young people used to do whatever they wanted. "Don't trust anyone over 30!" they said.

In the arts, people like Andy Warhol created "pop art." And fashions changed, too. The mini-skirt became popular, and then the "unisex" look followed. Young people started wearing blue jeans everywhere – to school, fancy restaurants, and concerts. Many of them had very long hair and wore lots of rings, beads, and bracelets. In music, the most popular group was the Beatles. Their songs told the story of the sixties. They sang about love, peace, and personal freedom.

2 Now find the best place in each paragraph for these sentences.

Paragraph 1: Others remember it for the Civil Rights Movement and the peace marches.

Paragraph 2: He painted pictures of everyday objects like soup cans.

2 I'm just passing through

1 SNAPSHOT

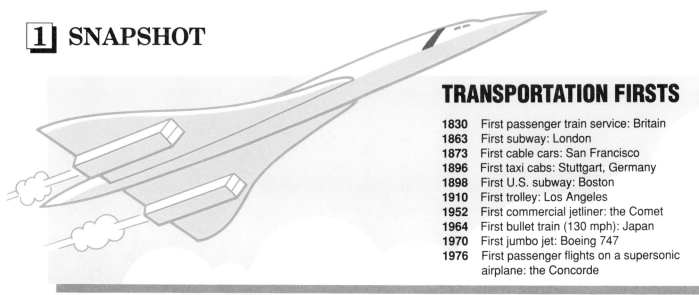

TRANSPORTATION FIRSTS

1830	First passenger train service: Britain
1863	First subway: London
1873	First cable cars: San Francisco
1896	First taxi cabs: Stuttgart, Germany
1898	First U.S. subway: Boston
1910	First trolley: Los Angeles
1952	First commercial jetliner: the Comet
1964	First bullet train (130 mph): Japan
1970	First jumbo jet: Boeing 747
1976	First passenger flights on a supersonic airplane: the Concorde

Discussion

How many of these kinds of transportation have you traveled on?

Is transportation a problem in your city? If so, why?

How many different forms of transportation does it take to get from your school to (a) your home, (b) your workplace or college, and (c) the nearest airport?

2 CONVERSATION

1 Listen and practice.

A: Excuse me, officer. Could you tell me how often the number 6 bus comes?

B: You just missed it, ma'am, but there's another one in half an hour.

A: Oh, no! Then could you tell me where Adam Street is?

B: Two blocks east and one block north, ma'am.

A: Thank you. And just one more thing. Do you know where the nearest restroom is?

B: Right behind you, ma'am. See that sign?

A: Oh! Thanks a lot.

2 Now listen and mark these places on the map.

a) bus station   d) subway entrance

b) taxi stand   e) parking lot

c) bus stop

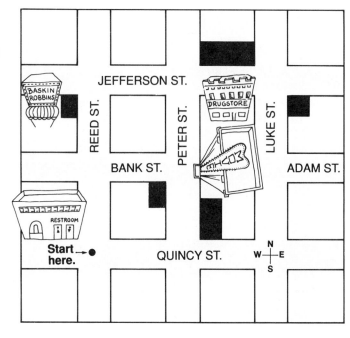

8

3 PRONUNCIATION: Question intonation 📼

1 Wh-questions usually have falling intonation:

How often does the bus come?

Where is the nearest taxi stand?

Indirect questions usually have rising intonation:

Can you tell me how often the bus comes?

Could you tell me where to catch the airport bus?

2 Now listen and practice.

Where is Adam Street?
Could you tell me where Adam Street is?
What time does the department store open?
Do you know what time the department store opens?

4 GRAMMAR FOCUS: Indirect questions from Wh-questions 📼

Wh-questions with *be*	Indirect questions
Where is the bank?	Could you tell me **where the bank is?**
Where is Oak Street?	Do you know **where Oak Street is?**

Wh-questions with *do*	Indirect questions
How often does the bus come?	Can you tell me **how often the bus comes?**
When do the banks open?	Do you know **when the banks open?**
What time does the market close?	Do you know **what time the market closes?**

1 Make indirect questions from these Wh-questions.

a) How much does a taxi to the airport cost?
b) Where is the nearest subway station?
c) What time does the last bus come?
d) When do the government offices open?
e) Where is the train station?
f) How often does the airport bus leave?
g) Where are some good restaurants around here?

2 Now write four indirect questions about things in your city.

3 *Pair work* Take turns asking your questions. Use rising intonation.

5 WORD POWER: City landmarks

1 Arrange these places into the lists below.

The American Express Office
The City Hall
The Concert Hall
The IBM Building
The Immigration Department
The Main Post Office
The National Gallery
The Science Museum
The South Point Shopping Plaza

Commercial buildings

Government office buildings

Arts and entertainment centers

2 *Pair work* Now add the names of two places in your city to each list.

3 *Class activity* What are the most important landmarks in your city?

6 CONVERSATION 📼

1 Listen and practice.

A: Excuse me, please. Do you know where the nearest bank is?
B: Well, the City Bank isn't far from here. Do you know where the Main Post Office is?
A: No, not really. I'm just passing through.
B: Well, first go down this street to the traffic light.
A: OK.
B: Then turn left and go west on Sunset Boulevard for about two blocks. The bank is on your right, just past the post office.
A: All right. Thanks!
B: You're welcome.

2 Now listen to the rest of the conversation. Who did the man call? Why?

7 GRAMMAR FOCUS: Sequence markers and imperatives

> **First, go** down this street to the signal.
> **Next, turn** right and **go** east on King Street for about two blocks.
> **Then look** for the Sears Building.
> **After that, go** up the little street beside it.
> **Finally, cross** the bridge and you're there.

Number the sentences from 1 to 11 to make a conversation.
Then practice it with a partner.

A

.... Did you say Blade Street?
.... I'm trying to find La Taverna Restaurant.
...1... Excuse me, I'm lost.
.... OK. Thanks very much.
.... To the traffic light, OK.
.... On Henderson Avenue. Could you
tell me how to get there, please?

B

.... Well, first go along Nathan Road to the
traffic light.
.... Oh, I know where that is. It's on
Henderson Avenue.
.... No, Blake Street. Go down Blake until you
get to Henderson. La Taverna is on the left.
.... After that, cross the street and then go
down Blake Street.
.... Oh, what are you looking for?

8 HERE AND THERE

Pair work Take turns giving directions to these
or other places near your class.

a post office	a supermarket	a bar
a drycleaner's	a coffee shop	a bank

A: I'm trying to find . . . Is there one around here?
B: Yes, there's one on . . . Street. Let me tell you
how to get there. First, . . .

Useful words

across
behind
up/down the street from
in front/back of
in the middle of the block on
near
next to
on
on the corner of
opposite

> ▶ **Interchange 2:**
> **Excuse me, I'm lost!**
>
> Can you find your way around
> town? Student A look at page 103
> and Student B at page 104.

Drawing by Stevenson; © 1976 The New Yorker Magazine, Inc.

9 LISTENING 📼

1 Martin is explaining how to get to his house. Listen and number five
of the pictures from 1 to 5 in the order you hear them.

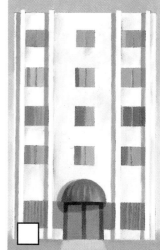

2 Now listen to the conversation again and take notes.

3 *Pair work* Use your notes and describe how to get to Martin's house.

10 WRITING

1 Write directions to get to your home from this class.

I live at 1315 Cedar Drive. The best way to get there is by bus. First, take a number 16 bus on 22nd Street, and get off at Columbia and Beach. Then...

I live in Garden City. To get there by car, first take Highway 205 West and get off on Delta Street. Go north on Delta until you come to the second traffic light, and then...

2 *Pair work* Take turns reading your directions.
Your partner takes notes or draws a map.

3 Now use your notes or map and check the directions to your partner's
home like this.

OK. You live at 1315 Cedar Drive.
First, I take a number 16 bus ...

11 READING: San Francisco

Read about this walking tour of San Francisco and draw the route on the map.

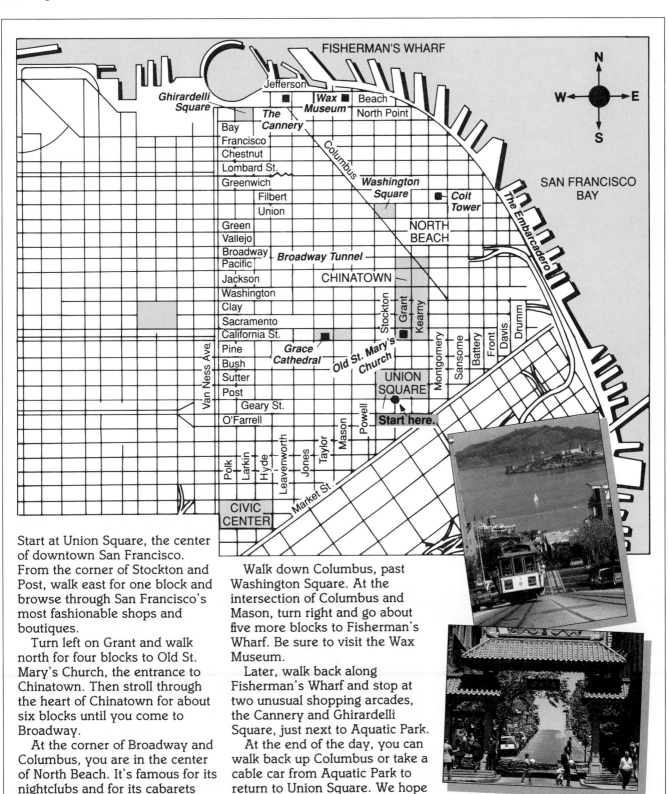

Start at Union Square, the center of downtown San Francisco. From the corner of Stockton and Post, walk east for one block and browse through San Francisco's most fashionable shops and boutiques.

Turn left on Grant and walk north for four blocks to Old St. Mary's Church, the entrance to Chinatown. Then stroll through the heart of Chinatown for about six blocks until you come to Broadway.

At the corner of Broadway and Columbus, you are in the center of North Beach. It's famous for its nightclubs and for its cabarets and Italian cafes.

Walk down Columbus, past Washington Square. At the intersection of Columbus and Mason, turn right and go about five more blocks to Fisherman's Wharf. Be sure to visit the Wax Museum.

Later, walk back along Fisherman's Wharf and stop at two unusual shopping arcades, the Cannery and Ghirardelli Square, just next to Aquatic Park.

At the end of the day, you can walk back up Columbus or take a cable car from Aquatic Park to return to Union Square. We hope you enjoy the tour!

3 That's outrageous!

1 WORD POWER: Houses

1 Where would you find these things in a house or an apartment? Write them on the floor plan below, in the room where they belong. Then compare with a partner.

carpet
closet
coffee table
couch
cupboard
shower
sink

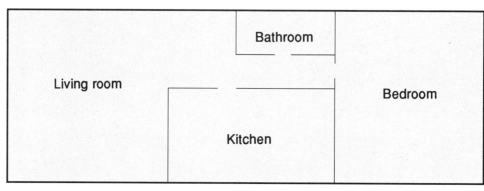

Living room

Bathroom

Bedroom

Kitchen

2 *Pair work* Now add six more words to the floor plan. Write them in the room where they belong.

2 CONVERSATION 🔲

1 Listen and practice.

A: Hello?
B: Hello, Mr. Andrews? This is Max from Ripley's Realty.
A: Hi. Have you found a house for me yet?
B: Yes, I have a great house to show you on Padley Drive. It's only $200,000.
A: Oh, that's too expensive for me.
B: Well, I have another one on Bank Street. It's only $85,000. But it only has one bedroom.
A: Oh, that's not big enough.
B: Well, how about a house in the country?
A: That sounds interesting.
B: Yes, it's fairly old, so it needs a little work. But it's really nice, and it has a lovely view.

RIPLEY REALTY $

FIXER-UPPER

2 Listen to the rest of the conversation. What else does the realtor say about the house?

14

3 GRAMMAR FOCUS: Adverbs and adjectives 📼

It's **very** small.	It's **not very** big.
awfully	It's big **enough.**
really	It's **not** big **enough.**
pretty	It's **too** small.
fairly	

1 Write sentences that have similar meanings to the sentences below. Use the grammar box above and the words in the list below.

My apartment is too small.   *It's not big enough.*   or

It's not very big.

a) This neighborhood is not clean enough.
b) The downtown area is not safe at night.
c) My apartment is not very expensive.
d) It's too warm here in the summer.
e) This is a nice city to live in.

big	dirty
cheap	exciting
clean	hot
cool	interesting
dangerous	pleasant

2 Now match these questions with suitable responses.

a) What's the weather like in your hometown?
b) Do you live in a nice neighborhood?
c) What's your house or apartment like?
d) What's your city like to live in?

.... It's fairly small, but it's in a good neighborhood.
.... It's very cold in the winter, but it's pretty nice in the summer.
.... It's very crowded, and it's too polluted.
.... It's pretty comfortable, and the rent is reasonable, too.
.... It's expensive to live here, but it's a really exciting place.
.... It's all right, but it's too far from my office downtown.
.... It's pretty nice, and the people are very friendly, too.

3 Write six sentences to describe your home, neighborhood, or city. Then compare with a partner.

4 WHAT'S IT LIKE?

Pair work   Take turns talking about one of these places.

What's your favorite city like?
      hometown
What's it like there?
What's the cost of living like?
What's the transportation like?
How's the weather there?
Is it . . . (exciting, fun)?
What's the nightlife like?

Do you live in a house or an apartment?
What's it like?
Is it . . . (quiet, comfortable)?
How . . . (big, old, safe) is it?
What's the neighborhood like?

What do you like most about it?
What don't you like about it?

5 LISTENING 🔲

Orange City. High-rise studio. $875. Phone Mr. Marsh 893-5340.	**Parkwood Gardens.** 1-bdrm. apt. Pool. $550. 894-4621 eves.	**2 bedroom home** near hospital. $925. 563-7613.
Large sunny room in quiet house on Elm Ave. Share utilities. $260. Call Sheri at 864-3664.	**Spring St. apt.** 2 bedrooms with view. Partly furnished. $680/mo. 567-4496.	**In Newton Square.** 3-BR 2-bath house w/garden. $1,200. 672-1246.

1 Listen to people calling about three of the ads above. Number the ads from 1 to 3 in the order you hear them.

2 Now listen again and take notes. What other information do you hear about each place?

6 SNAPSHOT

CITY TO CITY

In Washington, D.C., no building may be taller than
   the Capitol Building.
The uniforms worn by the Swiss Guards in Vatican City
   were designed by Michelangelo in the early sixteenth century.
In Venice, Italy, there are more than 400 bridges.
Bangkok, Thailand, is sometimes called "Venice of the East"
   because of its many canals.
The largest town in area is Mount Isa, Queensland,
   Australia, with 15,822 square miles.
Mexico City is sinking by 6-8 inches a year.
The modern city of Amsterdam consists of 90 islands.
The name "Hong Kong" means "fragrant harbor" in Chinese.

Discussion
Do you know anything else about the cities above?
Name two unusual facts about a city in your country.

7 CONVERSATION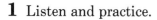

1 Listen and practice.

Client: Hotels are really expensive in Bangkok!

Agent: Yes, but not as expensive as Tokyo. I just paid $150 a night there!

Client: That's outrageous!

Agent: Yes, it is.

Client: But which is more interesting?

Agent: Well, Tokyo has good sightseeing, but Bangkok's much more fun, especially at night!

2 Now close your books and practice the conversation again.

3 Listen to the rest of the conversation. What does the travel agent say about nightlife in Bangkok?

8 GRAMMAR FOCUS: Comparisons with adjectives

With adjective + *er*	**With *more/less* + adjective**
Tokyo is **bigger than** Bangkok.	Tokyo is **more crowded than** Bangkok.
Bangkok is **(much) smaller.**	Bangkok is **(much) less crowded.**
Bangkok is **not as big as** Tokyo.	Tokyo is **not as polluted as** Bangkok.
It's **not as modern.**	It's **not as cheap.**

1 Use two words to complete each of these sentences. (See page 133 for comparative forms.)

a) London is more .... Lisbon. (expensive)

b) Public transportation in Toronto is .... in Los Angeles. (good)

c) Honolulu is much less .... Hong Kong. (crowded)

d) São Paulo is much .... Brasília. (large)

e) The weather in Portland is not as .... in San Diego. (nice)

f) Ottawa is much .... in winter .... Vancouver. (cold)

g) San Francisco is not as .... in summer .... New York. (hot)

2 Now write six sentences like these about cities you know and then compare with a partner.

17

9 PRONUNCIATION: Sentence stress 🔊

1 We stress words that carry the most important information.

Tokyo is **bigger** than **Bangkok. Bangkok** is **not** as **big** as **Tokyo.**

2 Now listen and practice the sentences you completed in Exercise 8.1.

10 WHAT'S THE DIFFERENCE?

1 *Pair work* Choose two cities in your country or two other cities you know. How are they different? Discuss some of these topics.

size	transportation	housing	entertainment	food
weather	cost of living	people	shopping	problems

A: Let's compare Paris and ...
B: All right. And let's talk about food first.
A: OK. I think the food in Paris is ...
B: Yeah, and ...

2 *Class activity* Tell the class which cities you compared and how many differences you found.

11 WRITING

1 Write about the cities you compared in Exercise 10 or two other places you know about.

> There are several differences between San Francisco and Miami. San Francisco has better transportation than Miami. But Miami has nicer beaches, and ...

2 *Pair work* Exchange compositions. Ask your partner questions about his or her composition.

12 LISTENING 🔊

Listen and choose the correct response.

a) .... Yes, Ottawa is bigger.
   .... Yes, it is.

b) .... Brazil is bigger.
   .... No, it's not as big.

c) .... Yes, much warmer.
   .... Yes, much smaller.

d) .... Yes, much hotter.
   .... Yes, it's more expensive.

e) .... Yes, much more difficult.
   .... No, it's not as old.

f) .... Yes, it's not as good.
   .... Yes, it's much better.

13 READING: Apartments for sale

1 Read these newspaper ads and find five differences between the apartment complexes.

SPRING GARDEN

The Spring Garden Apartment Complex offers you and your family country living at its best. Surrounded by beautiful woods and hills, Spring Garden is located ten miles outside the city but is only minutes from downtown on the freeway.

Unfurnished two-bedroom apartments are available. Each apartment has a dishwasher, central heating, air conditioning, and a laundry room. Children and pets are welcome.

In addition, there are tennis and basketball courts, two swimming pools, and a playground. There are two parking spaces for each apartment.

REGENCY TOWERS

Come and experience the luxury of **Regency Towers** and enjoy the convenience of living only a five-minute walk from the city center!

Each apartment in this forty-story building has a wonderful view of the city. A wide choice of apartments is available, from studios to large three-bedroom apartments.

Each apartment is completely furnished and offers every modern convenience: central heating, air conditioning, laundry facilities, and your own microwave oven. Free maid service is available. Adults preferred; no pets. Regency Towers also offers a swimming pool and an exercise room. There is twenty-four-hour security service.

2 Find words in the passage that mean:

a) very comfortable and with an expensive feeling
b) area with many trees
c) a group of buildings

3 Which complex would you prefer to live in? Why?

▶ **Interchange 3: Housing survey**

Where do your classmates live? Find out about their homes with the survey on page 105.

Review of Units 1-3

1 Conversation

Pair work   Take turns talking about yourself.

A: So, can I ask you a few questions about yourself?
B: ...
A: Where did you grow up?
B: ...
A: Uh-huh. And did you go to high school there?
B: ...
A: Really? What sports did you use to play in high school?
B: ...
A: Oh, yeah? Did you have a part-time job when you were a teenager?
B: ...
A: So when did you graduate from high school?
B: ...
A: And what did you do after that?
B: ...

2 How times have changed!

1 *Group work*   Take turns talking about how family life has changed in the last fifty years in your country. Ask questions like these.

How big were families fifty years ago? How about today?
What kinds of homes did people live in then?
What kinds of jobs did men use to have? And what about women?
How were schools different?
Did everyone go to high school?
How much did people earn then?
What kinds of machines and appliances did people use?
How did they do household chores?
How did they use to travel to work?

2 *Class activity*   Compare answers. Do you think life was better in the old days? Why or why not?

3 Listening 📼

Listen to people asking for information, and choose the correct response.

a) .... It's just around the corner.
.... Yes, it closes at 3:00.

b) .... Yes, it does.
.... The next one is in ten minutes.

c) .... On the corner of Main and 15th.
.... At nine o'clock in the morning.

d) .... It's in the shopping center on King Street.
.... Not until two o'clock.

e) .... Yes, in the Fairmont Hotel on Main Street.
.... Yes, I do.

f) .... By bus.
.... On the corner of Orange and Dewey.

4 Where am I going?

1 *Pair work* Think of a well-known building or place (e.g., a bank, restaurant, office building, department store) within walking distance of your class. Write down the easiest way to get there from class.

First, go outside and turn left. Then walk three blocks to the traffic light. Go south on ...

End your directions like this (but don't give the name of the place).

It's a large gray building on the corner of 1st and Elm. You can't miss it!

2 *Class activity* Read your directions to the class. Other students try to guess the name of the building or place.

5 Differences

1 *Pair work* Choose one of these pairs and compare them. How many differences can you think of?

a restaurant and a fast food restaurant
a street market and a department store

Talk about them like this.

People are more friendly in a ...
You don't use a credit card in a ...
Prices are cheaper in a ...
It's more expensive in a ...

2 *Class activity* Compare the differences.

4 I've never heard of that!

1 SNAPSHOT

ETHNIC FAVORITES

Baked Fettucine (Italy): a pasta dish cooked with butter, cheese, and cream

Beggar's Chicken (China): chicken, mushrooms, and vegetables, wrapped in paper and clay, and baked

Devonshire Scones (Great Britain, New Zealand): small baked buns made of flour, butter, and milk, served with whipped cream and jam

Feijoada (Brazil): a traditional dish made of black beans, garlic, spices, and pork

Gado Gado (Indonesia): a salad made with sliced vegetables, eggs, and a thick peanut sauce

Moussaka (Greece): a baked dish with ground lamb, tomatoes, eggplant, cheese, and a white sauce

Complete the information below. Then compare with a partner.

My favorite food:

Food I really don't like:

The most unusual food I've ever eaten:

Discussion

How often do you eat out? What do you usually order?

2 CONVERSATION 🔊

1 Listen and practice.

A: Hey, this sounds good – snails with garlic. Have you ever eaten snails?

B: No, I haven't.

A: Oh, they're delicious! I had them last time. Like to try some?

B: No, thanks. They sound strange.

C: Have you decided on an appetizer yet?

A: Yes. I'll have the snails, please.

C: And you, sir?

B: I think I'll have the fried brains.

A: Fried brains? Now that sounds strange!

2 Now listen to the rest of the conversation.

How did the man like the fried brains?
What else did he order?

22

3 GRAMMAR FOCUS: Past tense and present perfect 🔊

Past tense: completed events at a definite time in the past	Present perfect: events within a time period up to the present

Did you **eat** snails at the restaurant last night?
   Yes, I **did.**
Did you **go** to Italy last summer?
   No, I **didn't.**
I **went** to a Thai restaurant on Saturday.
	Have you **(ever) eaten** snails?
	   Yes, I **have.**
	Have you **been** to Italy?
	   No, I **haven't.**
	I **have never been** to a Thai restaurant.

1 Complete these conversations and then practice them with a partner.
(See page 133 for verb forms.)

a) A: Have you ever .... (be) on a rollercoaster?
   B: Yes, I .... It was fun!
b) A: Did you .... (go) to the movies last weekend?
   B: No, I .... I was too busy.
c) A: Did you .... (take) a vacation last year?
   B: Yes, I .... I went skiing.
d) A: Have you .... (take) a vacation this year?
   B: No, I .... Not yet.
e) A: Have you ever .... (try) Mexican food?
   B: Yes, I .... It's delicious!
f) A: Did you .... (do) the homework yesterday?
   B: No, I .... Can I look at yours?

2 *Pair work* Now take turns asking the questions and giving your own information.

4 BUSYBODIES

Pair work Ask your partner these questions and four more of your own.

Did you . . . ?
learn how to type in high school
eat out last weekend
do anything interesting last night
drive to class today

Have you ever . . . ?
eaten frog's legs
flown in a helicopter
gone skiing
been to a fortune teller

5 LISTENING 🔊

1 Listen to a woman talking about what happened in a restaurant.
Why did she go there?   Who did she see?   What happened?

2 Has anything like this ever happened to you?

6 WORD POWER

1 *Pair work* Write these words on the chart below.
Then add eight more words to the chart.

| cabbage | ice cream | onion | saucepan | tablespoon |
| cheesecake | potato chips | peanuts | soda | tomato juice |

Beverages	**Snacks**	**Vegetables**	**Desserts**	**Utensils**

2 Now use six of the words in sentences.

Have you ever tried chocolate cheesecake?

7 PRONUNCIATION: Word stress

1 Are these words stressed on the 1st or 2nd syllable? Mark the
stressed syllable. Then listen and check.

| banana | chicken | delicious | pizza | restaurant |
| beverage | coffee | dessert | potato | vacation |

2 Now listen and mark the stressed syllables in the words in Exercise 6.
Then take turns reading the words aloud with a partner, and check the
correct stress.

8 CONVERSATION

1 Listen and practice.

A: What's your favorite snack?
B: Oh, it's a sandwich with peanut butter, honey,
   and a banana. It's really delicious!
A: Ugh! I've never heard of that! How do you make it?
B: Well, first, you take two pieces of bread and
   spread peanut butter on them. Then cut up a
   banana into small slices and put them on one
   of the pieces of bread. Then pour some honey
   over the bananas and put the other piece of
   bread on top.
A: It sounds awful!

2 *Pair work* Now cover the conversation. Can you remember how to
make this unusual peanut butter sandwich?

9 GRAMMAR FOCUS: Two-part verbs 🔲

With nouns		With pronouns
Cut up the banana.	**Cut** the banana **up**.	**Cut** it **up**. (*Not:* Cut up it.)
Put in the sugar.	**Put** the sugar **in**.	**Put** it **in**. (*Not:* Put in it.)

1 Put the words in parentheses in suitable places in these sentences.
Then compare with a partner.

a) Pick some fresh fish and vegetables from the market and then put
   them the refrigerator until you are ready to cook. (up, in)
b) Get your cookbook and look the recipe. (out, up)
c) Turn the oven and set it at 300 degrees. (on)
d) Chop the vegetables and put them a pan. (up, in)
e) Put the fish a baking pan and pour the sauce it. (in, over)
f) Make sure you clean the kitchen when you are finished. (up)
g) Take the dishes of the dishwasher and put them the cupboard. (out, in)

2 *Pair work* Complete this recipe with the two-part verbs below.
Some of them can be used more than once.

chop up	pour on	put on	take out
cut up	put in	take off	turn over

Barbecued Kebobs

a) First, ... some wood and ....
   it .... the barbecue, or use some charcoal.
b) Then .... some lighter fluid .... and
   light the fire.
c) Now .... the meat and
   vegetables, and .... them .... a small
   bowl with some sauce.
d) .... them .... of the bowl after twenty minutes.
e) Then .... the meat and vegetables .... the
   skewers and .... them .... the barbecue.
f) .... the meat .... after ten minutes
   and cook it for 10–15 minutes more.
g) Then .... the kebobs .... the
   barbecue and enjoy!

10 LISTENING

Listen to people describing how to make the things below. One
ingredient in each description is wrong. Do you know what it is?

a) banana milkshake   b) chicken sandwich   c) vegetable salad   d) iced lemon tea

11 TEMPTING SNACKS

1 Make notes about your favorite snack.

What is it?
What ingredients do you need to make it?
How do you make it?

2 *Pair work*   Take turns describing
how to make your favorite snack.

A: What's your favorite snack?
B: It's . . .
A: What ingredients do you need to make it?
B: To make it you need . . .
A: How do you make it?
B: First, you . . .   After that, . . .   Next, . . .   Then . . .

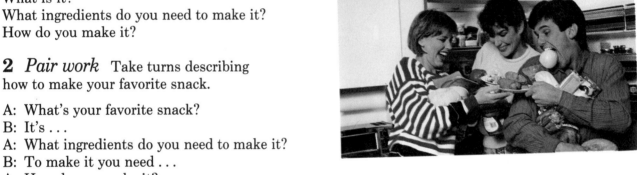

3 *Class activity*   Which students had interesting snacks? Tell the
class how to make them.

12 WRITING: Recipes

1 *Pair work*   Write a recipe for an interesting dish.
First, list the ingredients you need.
Then describe how to make the dish.

*This recipe is for chicken curry. For this
dish you need chicken, coconut milk, . . .*

*First, you cut up the chicken, and then fry
the chicken pieces lightly in oil . . .*

2 *Group work*   Exchange recipes and read them.
Is there a recipe you would like to try?

▶ **Interchange 4: Risky business**

Here's a chance to be nosy! Turn to page 106.

13 READING: The worst place for a meal

1 Read these statements. Do you think they are true (**T**) or false (**F**)?

a) Standard airplane meals are high in calories and fat.
b) Most people don't enjoy eating when they fly.
c) Roast beef with gravy is a healthier choice for a meal than seafood.
d) You can order special meals from airlines.

2 Now read the passage and check your answers.

A typical airline breakfast is a cheese omelet, croissant, bacon, and danish. That's at least 900 calories, which is more than many people eat in a day and about twice as much as most people eat for breakfast.

Other typical airline meals include buttered vegetables, fried foods, and meats served with gravy. Although travelers complain about airline food, most of them eat everything that is put in front of them.

What can you do to avoid unhealthy foods on an airplane? First, ask the airline what special meals they serve. Many serve vegetarian, kosher, and other types of special meals if you give them advance notice. Second, bring your own snack on board! Some fruit or a bag of popcorn purchased at the airport is much lower in fat and calories than the peanuts they give you. Third, if you have a choice between meat and seafood, choose the seafood. And finally, drink milk, juice, or club soda instead of an alcoholic beverage. You'll feel much better when you get off the plane!

3 *Pair work* Find words in the passage that mean:

a) a flaky, rich, buttery roll   b) a thick sauce   c) contains no meat

5 Going places

1 SNAPSHOT

Discussion

What are five cities in North America you would most like to visit?

What are the five most popular cities and places in your country for foreign visitors?

What are the three places you would most like to visit in the world?

TRAVEL FACTS

The five most popular destinations for U.S. travelers:
Canada, Mexico, Great Britain, West Germany, France

The five most popular cities in the U.S. for foreign visitors:
New York City, Los Angeles, San Francisco, Honolulu, Miami

Average amount spent by visitors to the U.S.:
Australians $1,296, Japanese $960, Canadians $291

The most frequent item taken by guests from the Plaza Hotel, New York: *bathrobes (200 a month)*

2 WORD POWER: Travel

1 *Pair work* Add these words to the word map.

backpack	medication	plane tickets	Swiss Army knife	vaccination
credit card	money belt	shorts	tent	visa
health insurance	passport	sleeping bag	traveler's checks	windbreaker

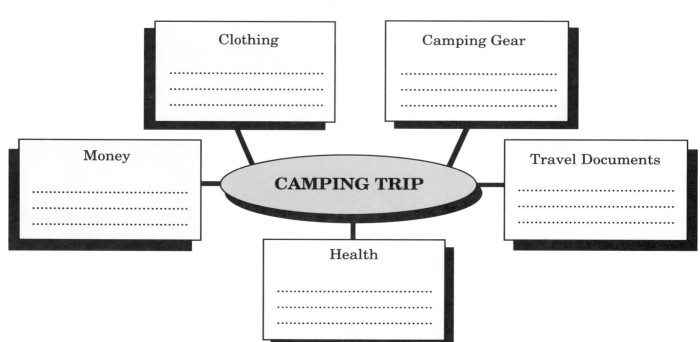

Clothing
....
....
....

Camping Gear
....
....
....

Money
....
....
....

CAMPING TRIP

Travel Documents
....
....
....

Health
....
....
....

2 Now add five more words to the map. Then compare with other students.

28

3 CONVERSATION 🔊

1 Listen and practice.

A: Hey, Mom. I'm thinking of hitchhiking around Europe this summer. What do you think?

B: Hitchhiking? That sounds dangerous! You shouldn't go by yourself. You ought to go with a friend.

A: Yes, I've thought of that.

B: And you'd better talk to your father first.

A: I did already. He thinks it's a great idea. He wants to come with me!

2 *Class activity* Have you ever been hitchhiking? Would you like to hitchhike in Europe? Where?

4 GRAMMAR FOCUS: Modals for necessity and suggestions 🔊

Describing necessity	Giving suggestions
You **have to** get a visa.	You**'d better** talk to your father.
You **must** take warm clothes.	You **ought to** go with a friend.
	You **should** take a sleeping bag.
You **don't have to** get a passport.	You **shouldn't** go by yourself.

1 Give advice for someone who is thinking of taking a vacation abroad. Then compare with a partner.

You must get a passport.
You shouldn't pack too many clothes.

a) . . . get a passport.
b) . . . pack too many clothes.
c) . . . buy a roundtrip ticket.
d) . . . make hotel reservations.
e) . . . get health insurance.
f) . . . check the weather.
g) . . . carry lots of cash.
h) . . . get traveler's checks.
i) . . . take a lot of luggage.
j) . . . check on visas.
k) . . . carry your wallet in a back pocket.

2 *Pair work* Give four more pieces of advice.

5 LISTENING 📼

Mike is planning to visit New York City. He is asking a New Yorker for advice. Listen and complete the chart.

Best time of the year	Things to see and do	Things to avoid

6 TIPS FOR TOURISTS

1 *Group work* What advice would you give tourists planning to visit your city or country?

What time of the year should they visit?
What kinds of clothing do you think they ought to bring?
Where should they stay?

What places should they visit?
What should they see?
Is there anything they shouldn't do?
What other advice would you give them?

2 *Class activity* Compare your suggestions.

7 CONVERSATION 📼

1 Listen and practice.

Yumi: Are you going to go to the Halloween party?
Greg: Sure. I love Halloween!
Yumi: What are you going to wear?
Greg: I'm going as Frankenstein. How about you?
Yumi: I'm going to go as the Bride of Frankenstein.
Greg: Hey, maybe we should go together.

2 *Class activity* You're going to go to a Halloween party. What are you going as?

---

8 PRONUNCIATION: Reduced form of *going to* 📼

1 Listen to how **going to** is reduced before a verb.

What are you **going to** do after class?   We're **going to** see a movie.

2 Listen to these sentences with the reduced form of **going to.** Then practice.

What are you going to do tonight?
Are you going to go to the ballgame on Saturday?
Where are you going to have dinner tonight?

---

9 GRAMMAR FOCUS: Present continuous and *going to* for future 📼

With present continuous	With *going to* + verb
What **are** you **doing** after class? I'm not **doing** much.	What **are** you **going to do** after class? I'm not **going to do** much.
Are you **doing** anything tonight? Yes, I'm **going** to a movie.	**Are** you **going to do** anything tonight? Yes, I'm **going to go** to a movie.

1 Complete these conversations with the present continuous or **going to.**

a) A: .... you .... (do) anything
after class?
B: Yes, I'm .... (do) some shopping
downtown. Would you like to come?

b) A: What .... you .... (do)
tomorrow night?
B: Nothing much. Why?
A: Well, some of us .... (take) the
teacher out for coffee. Would you like to join us?

c) A: What .... you .... (do) on
Saturday?
B: Well, I .... (work) until four o'clock.
Then I .... (go) to a party. What
about you?
A: I'm .... (go) away for the weekend.

2 *Pair work* Practice the conversations above with
a partner. Use the reduced form of **going to** + verb.

3 Now have conversations about these times:

tonight, on Saturday night, on Sunday

31

10 LISTENING 📼

1 Dan is going to take a trip to Central and South America. Listen to his travel plans and number the countries he is going to visit from 1 to 6 in the order you hear them.

.... Argentina
.... Brazil
.... Chile
.... Colombia
.... Costa Rica
.... Ecuador
.... Nicaragua
.... Venezuela

2 Listen again. How good is Dan's Spanish? How long is he going to be away?

11 DREAM VACATION

1 *Pair work* You won some money in a lottery. Plan an interesting trip around the world. Discuss these questions and others of your own. Make notes.

Where are we going to start from?
What time of the year should we travel?
How are we going to travel?
How many countries and cities are we going to visit?
How long should we spend in each place?
Where are we going to stay?
What are we planning to do and see there?
How much money should we take?
What things do we need to take?

2 *Group work* Compare your plans. Which trip sounds the most exciting?

12 WRITING: Itineraries

1 Write about the trip you planned in Exercise 11 or a real trip you plan to take.

Next summer I'm planning to take a rafting trip down the Colorado River in the Grand Canyon. I'm going with a group of friends from school and ...

▶ **Interchange 5: Coastal fling**

Plan an interesting vacation on the coast. Student A look at page 107 and Student B at page 108.

2 *Class activity* Put your compositions on the bulletin board. Which trip would you like to take?

13 READING: Fitness in the air

1 Many people get jet lag when they travel. Here are some exercises you can do in your seat on a long plane flight that will reduce jet lag. Match each exercise with the correct picture.

a) Turn your head to the left and touch your shoulder with your chin. Then repeat to the right.

b) Bend your back slightly, then drop your head back so that you can see the overhead compartment. Relax your jaw. Feel the stretch in your neck and chin.

c) Sit up straight and lift your left foot off the floor, raising your whole leg about an inch off the seat. Turn your foot to the right and then to the left ten times. Repeat with the right foot.

d) Sit up straight with your shoulders slightly forward. Put your fingers together and raise your arms to chest level, keeping your elbows straight and your palms facing outward. Stretch and then relax.

e) Sit up straight. Hold the right armrest with your left hand and turn your body and head to the right. Release and then hold the left armrest with your right hand and turn to the left.

2 *Pair work* Take turns. Read an exercise aloud to your partner. He or she will follow your instructions.

6 Sure! No problem!

1 WHAT WAS THAT? 📼

Pedro is having trouble getting to sleep. Listen to five noises that are keeping him awake. What do you think is happening?

#1
A: It sounds like some kind of machine.
B: I think it sounds like someone is drilling in the street.

2 CONVERSATION 📼

1 Match each request with the correct response below.

a) Would you mind turning down the radio, André? It's very loud.

b) Hey, Yoko! Could you move your car? It's blocking my driveway.

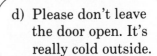

d) Please don't leave the door open. It's really cold outside.

c) Would you mind not smoking here? This is a nonsmoking section.

.... OK. I'll put it out.   .... Sure. No problem.
.... All right. I'll close it.   .... Oh, OK. I'll park it across the street.

2 Now listen and check. Then practice with a partner.

3 GRAMMAR FOCUS: Requests with imperatives and modals 🔲

Turn the TV **down**.	**Can** you **turn** the TV **down?**
Leave the door **open**.	**Could** you **leave** the door **open**, please?
Please **keep** the noise **down**.	**Would** you please **keep** the noise **down?**
Move your car, please.	**Would** you **mind moving** your car?
Please **don't park** here.	**Would** you **mind not parking** here, please?

1 Match each request with a suitable response.
Then compare with a partner and practice.

a) Would you mind mailing these letters for me?
b) Excuse me. Could you move your bag, please?
c) Would you mind not smoking here?
d) Please try to come to class on time.

.... I'm sorry. I won't be late again. I promise!
.... OK. I'll go outside.
.... All right. I'll do it when I go downtown this afternoon.
.... Sure! No problem!
.... Sorry. I didn't know it was bothering you.
.... I'm sorry, but it's not mine.

2 *Pair work* Now take turns making the requests again.
This time give your own responses.

3 Use these cues to make requests.
Then compare with a partner.

a) . . . lend me a dollar
b) . . . get me a cup of coffee
c) . . . open the window
d) . . . turn off the light
e) . . . help me move to my new
      apartment tomorrow
f) . . . take your feet off my chair
g) . . . blow smoke in my face

4 PRONUNCIATION: Reduced forms 🔲

1 Listen to the reduced forms in these requests.

Could you pass me my bag?   **Would you** turn on the air conditioner?

Could you put that away?   **Would you** turn off the VCR?

2 *Pair work* Take turns making the requests you wrote in
Exercise 3.3 and giving responses. Pay attention to reduced forms.

5 NO PROBLEM!

1 Think of six interesting or unusual requests you want to make to your classmates and the teacher.

2 *Class activity* Go around the class and make your requests. How many people accepted and how many refused?

Accepting a request

Oh, sure. I'd be glad to!
OK. I'll do that.
All right.
Sure! No problem!

Refusing a request

Oh, sorry. I can't right now.
I'm sorry, but I'm busy.
I'd rather not.
What? You must be kidding!

6 LISTENING 📼

Listen to requests and choose the correct response.

a) .... Yes, in a minute.
.... Yes, it is.

b) .... Yes, it's very loud.
.... All right.

c) .... Sure. Diet or regular?
.... Oh, sorry.

d) .... Oh, of course.
.... Yours or mine?

e) .... No, thanks.
.... Sorry, I'm using it.

f) .... Oh, I'm sorry.
.... I am, too.

7 WORD POWER: Two-part verbs

1 Find nouns that can be used with these two-part verbs. Then compare with a partner.

a) clean up   .... the books   .... your tie
b) hang up   .... the cat   .... the toys
c) pick up   .... your cigarette   .... the trash
d) put away   .... your clothes   .... the TV
e) put on   .... your coat   .... the yard
f) put out   .... the faucet
g) take off   .... the light
h) take out   .... the phone
i) turn down   .... the radio
j) turn off   .... a record
k) turn on   .... the room
l) turn up   .... your shoes

2 *Pair work* Now make requests using four of the verbs above.

8 SNAPSHOT

APOLOGIES

People make apologies in different ways.
For example, if you are late for work, you can. . .

apologize "I'm sorry I'm late."
apologize and. . .
  explain "I missed the bus."
  say you made a mistake "I forgot to check my bus schedule."
  offer to do something "I'll work late tonight."
  make a promise "I won't be late again."

In North America, people usually apologize and explain,
or apologize and offer to do something about it.

Discussion
How do people usually apologize in your country?
How would you apologize in these situations?
- You didn't answer a friend's letter.
- You didn't go to a friend's birthday party.

9 MAKING COMPLAINTS

1 Listen to how we can make complaints and respond to them.

Making a complaint

You're late! I've been waiting for an hour!   → Gee, I'm sorry. I missed the bus.
This library book was due back yesterday.   → Oh, sorry. I didn't realize it was overdue.

Apologizing and giving an explanation

Making a complaint

Excuse me, but your car is blocking my driveway. → I'm really sorry. I'll move it right away.
I think you've given me the wrong change.   → Sorry. Let me check the bill again.

Apologizing and offering to do something

2 Now choose the best response for each complaint. Then compare with a partner and practice them.

Complaints

a) By the way, I asked you to return my book to the library.

b) Don't forget you still owe me $20.

c) Hey, I need my cassette player back. Have you finished with it?

d) I was waiting for you at the coffee shop last night, but you didn't turn up. How come?

Responses

.... Sorry. They weren't there.

.... Oh, I got there late, and you were already gone. I'm really sorry.

.... Gosh, I'm sorry. Could I give them to you tomorrow?

.... Oh, gee, I'm sorry. Let me write you a check right now.

.... Oh, yeah. It's in my locker. I'll go and get it. Sorry.

.... Oh, sorry. I completely forgot about it. I'll take it back today.

3 Write responses to these complaints. Then compare with a partner and practice.

a) Your radio is too loud. I'm trying to study.

b) Look! The cover of this book wasn't torn when I lent it to you.

c) You've had my tennis racquet for over a month! Can I have it back?

d) You've left the room in a real mess!

---

10 BY THE WAY . . .

1 Think of four things you want to complain to people about and write complaints about each one.

Why don't you ever replace the cap on the toothpaste tube?

2 *Class activity* Now take turns complaining. Your classmates respond.

---

11 LISTENING

Listen to three people complaining. Which excuse do they get?

a) .... Kim's car broke down.
   .... The traffic was bad.

b) .... The restaurant is short of staff.
   .... The waiter is new on the job.

c) .... Bob bakes delicious cookies.
   .... There wasn't anything else to eat.

12 READING: Letters to the editor

1 Read these letters to a newspaper.

June 16

Waiting Forever

The other day I was waiting for Bus #2 and it didn't come for over an hour! This is the second time this month it's happened to me. And another thing. The bus drivers are rude these days. They don't wait for people to sit down before they start the bus. What does the bus company have to say about this?

Fed Up

Noise Pollution

I go to the city parks to relax and watch the birds. But these days the parks are full of people playing loud music. Why doesn't the city stop people from playing portable stereos in public so the rest of us can enjoy some peace and quiet?

Disappointed

Bad Marks for the Post Office

I'd like to complain about the poor service in the post office lately. Yesterday, I waited 25 minutes in line to buy a stamp. And then the clerk was very angry when I tried to buy a 40-cent stamp with a $20 bill. Doesn't the post office train its staff on how to be polite?

Angry Taxpayer

2 Which letters from June 16th are these letters replies to?

June 19

No Answer

I've had the same problem as your reader of June 16th. I called to get some information last week and I waited nearly 10 minutes before anyone answered the phone. And another thing. My mail always comes late these days!

Disgusted

Save the Beaches

I agree with your reader of June 16th. The noise at the beach is terrible, too. I hate going there nowadays. Why don't people use headphones?

Not Satisfied

13 WRITING: A letter to the editor

1 *Pair work* Write a letter of complaint to a newspaper about a problem in your city.

What is the problem?
Why does it bother you?
Where is it? What happens?
What should someone do about it?

2 *Class activity* Now put your letters on the bulletin board. Which ones do you agree with?

▶ **Interchange 6: That's no excuse!**

Find out how good you are at giving excuses. Student A look at page 109 and Student B at page 110.

Review of Units 4–6

1 Listening 📼

1 Listen to the Seasoned Chef describing a favorite recipe. Check (✓) the ingredients that you hear.

.... Curry powder   .... Milk
.... Celery   .... Peanuts
.... Water   .... Pepper
.... Lettuce   .... Rice
.... Mayonnaise   .... Walnuts

2 Listen again and write down the recipe.
Use these words: **boil, chop,** and **mix.**
Then compare with a partner.

2 Food for thought

1 *Pair work* Take turns asking these questions. If you answer "Yes," describe what happened.

Have you ever . . .

baked a cake?
made fried rice?
eaten sugar cane?
drunk coconut milk?
tried herbal tea?
eaten horse meat?
had rabbit?
tried brown rice?

not had enough money to pay for a check in a restaurant?
sent back a dish you ordered in a restaurant?
been to a barbecue?
been to a Mexican restaurant?
gone to a Greek restaurant?
been to a Thanksgiving dinner?
given a potluck party?

2 *Class activity* Now tell the class one interesting thing about your partner like this.

Anna went to San Francisco last year. She ordered a bowl of soup in a restaurant there, but she sent it back to the kitchen because there was a fly in her soup!

40

3 **Conversation:** The weekend

Pair work   Talk about your weekend plans. What are you going to do on Saturday afternoon, Saturday evening, and Sunday?

A: Do you have any plans for the weekend?
B: Yes, I'm going to be really busy.
A: Me, too. What are you going to do on Saturday?
B: . . . How about you?
A: . . .
B: Sounds fun! And how about Sunday?
A: I'm . . . What about you?
B: . . . Well, have a nice weekend!
A: . . .

4 **On the road**

1 *Group work*   Your friends are planning to take a long car trip on their next vacation.

What plans do they need to make?
How many suggestions can you think of?
Use **had better, must, ought to, should,** and **shouldn't.**

You should take some road maps.
You'd better check the tires on your car.
You shouldn't forget to bring a tent.

2 *Class activity*
Compare your suggestions.

5 **Sorry to remind you, but . . .**

1 *Pair work*   Cover each other's information.

Student A: Complain to your partner about these things:
- Your partner has not returned your tennis racquet.
- Your partner is playing a cassette very loudly. You are trying to study.
- Your partner has been using the telephone for twenty minutes. You need to make an urgent call.
- Your partner borrowed your typewriter. You need to use it.

Student B: Listen to your partner's complaints.
Apologize and make suitable responses.

2 Now change roles and find another partner.

7 What on earth is this?

1 SNAPSHOT

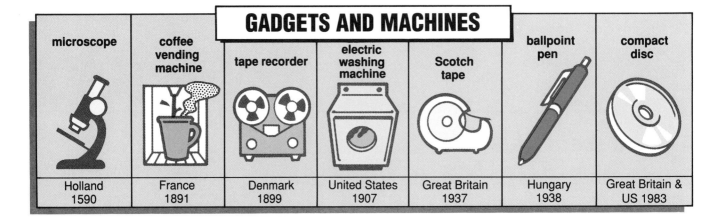

microscope	coffee vending machine	**GADGETS AND MACHINES**				ballpoint pen	compact disc
		tape recorder	electric washing machine	Scotch tape			
Holland 1590	France 1891	Denmark 1899	United States 1907	Great Britain 1937		Hungary 1938	Great Britain & US 1983

Complete the information below. Then compare with a partner.

The three most useful machines in my home:
The three most useful gadgets I own:
The most useless gadget I ever got:
The three most important inventions in the last 50 years:

2 CONVERSATION 📼

1 Listen and practice.

A: What on earth is this?
B: Oh, that's called a Musical Finder. It's the most wonderful new gadget on the market today!
A: Oh, what's it for?
B: It's used for finding things. And it's terrific! Look. You clip it on your glasses at night so you can find them in the morning. Then you just clap twice and you hear a tune. Listen.
A: Uh, I don't wear glasses. Thanks, anyway.

2 Listen to the rest of the conversation.

What else can you use the Musical Finder for?
What does the customer want to use it for?

3 WORD POWER: Countable and uncountable nouns

1 Arrange these countable nouns into the lists below and add two more words to each list.

brooms	a lighter	a pocketknife	a stapler
can openers	paper clips	a ruler	a vacuum cleaner

Office supplies　　　　*Gadgets*　　　　*Cleaning supplies*

2 Arrange these uncountable nouns into the lists below and add two more words to each list.

detergent	milk	soap	tea
glue	polish	tape	water

Office supplies　　　　*Beverages*　　　　*Cleaning supplies*

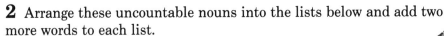

4 GRAMMAR FOCUS: Infinitives and gerunds after a preposition 📼

Infinitives	**Gerunds**
It's used **to find** things.	It's used **for finding** things.
You can use it **to make** things.	You can use it **for making** things.

1 Complete the phrases in column A with suitable information in column B. Then compare with a partner.

A

a) You can use scissors
b) You can use a Swiss Army knife
c) Glue is used
d) A blender is used
e) You can use pliers
f) A ruler is used

B

.... for fixing things.
.... to open cans.
.... to pull out nails.
.... for measuring things.
.... for cutting paper or cloth.
.... to make drinks.
.... to stick things together.
.... for cutting wire.

2 Now complete the phrases in A using your own information.

3 Write four questions about things in your home. Then take turns asking your questions.

What is a vacuum cleaner used for?

5 PRONUNCIATION: Stress in compound nouns 📼

1 In compound nouns, the first noun receives greater stress than the second. Listen and practice.

can opener **motor**cycle **pocket**knife
cigarette lighter **paper** clip **vacuum** cleaner

2 *Pair work* List six other compound nouns for household gadgets or appliances. Then say what they are used for.

6 LISTENING 📼

1 Listen to people talking about three of these gadgets.
Number the pictures from 1 to 3 in the order you hear them.

2 Listen again. What is each gadget used for?

7 THINGS IN COMMON

1 *Pair or group work* Find groups of words that have something in common. You can use the same words in more than one group. Make a list.

Chopsticks, a fork, and a knife are all used for eating.

a cassette tape	an envelope	a paper clip	soap	a television
a CD player	a fork	a radio	a stamp	a video
chopsticks	glue	a record	stationery	
detergent	a knife	shampoo	tape	

Useful expressions

. . . are all used to make things.   . . . are all used for making things.
. . . are all made of . . .   . . . are all kept in the . . .

2 Now compare your lists with another pair or group of students.

3 *Class activity* Who found the most groups of words?

8 CONVERSATION 📼

1 Listen and practice.

A: Good afternoon, sir. May I help you?
B: Uh, something's wrong with this watch.
A: What's the problem?
B: Well, it's stopped.
A: Oh? How long have you had it?
B: About a year.
A: OK. Let me have a look. Oh, the battery needs to be changed, and I think the watch needs cleaning. That's all!

2 *Pair work* Now close your books and practice the conversation again.

9 GRAMMAR FOCUS: Infinitives and gerunds 📼

Infinitives	Gerunds
The watch **needs to be cleaned.**	The watch **needs cleaning.**
The battery **needs to be changed.**	The battery **needs changing.**

1 Read about these problems and choose suitable suggestions. Then compare with a partner and practice.

a) These pants are too long.
b) These boots look terrible!
c) The cassette player won't work.
d) The lock on the door is broken.
e) My car sounds funny.
f) My suit looks awful!
g) The air conditioner isn't working right.

.... It needs to be fixed.
.... Maybe the batteries need changing.
.... They need to be shortened.
.... It probably needs to be serviced.
.... It needs checking.
.... They need to be polished.
.... It needs drycleaning.

2 *Pair work* Now look at these problems and make suggestions.

a) My motorcycle won't start.
b) I can't get the VCR to work right.
c) This room is a mess!
d) I dropped my watch and now it doesn't run.
e) The manager spilled coffee on his tie.

10 LISTENING 📼

Listen to two customers describing problems with things they bought.
What is the problem? What needs to be done?

11 FIXER UPPER

1 *Pair work* Look at these pictures of an apartment building and
one of its apartments. How many problems can you find?
What needs to be done?

Useful vocabulary

curtains	street lamp	mend
garbage	trash cans	mow
grass and weeds	windows	pick up
painting	fix	repair

2 *Group work* Now compare your suggestions.

---

12 WRITING

Someone is coming to your house to
repair something. You won't be home.
Write a note describing the problem.

▶ **Interchange 7:
But it's almost new!**

Have you ever taken anything back to
a store? Student A turn to page 111
and Student B to page 112.

The refrigerator isn't working right.
Would you mind taking a look at it?
I think the temperature control needs
checking. It doesn't seem to work.
It's too cold and everything freezes.

13 READING: Advertisements

1 Read these ads for unusual gadgets and match each ad with a picture.

The Peace Maker **$44.95**

Safe and Sound **$59.95**

Pocket Pal
$29.95

Blabbermouth **$12.95**

Security Bear **$79.95**

Keep your home safe from burglars with this "electric watchdog." When someone rings the doorbell, this gadget responds with angry dog barks. It's sure to keep strangers away from your home!

Now you can watch your favorite music as well as listen to it. This AM/FM radio will give you many hours of pleasure. Watch its lips move to the sounds of music or words. Crazy, but fun! Made of strong plastic.

Thieves can't bear this car alarm system. Just keep this cute stuffed animal in your car. If someone tries to break in, it will react with an ear-splitting siren. The thief won't stick around for long!

Does anyone snore or keep you awake? This can help! The sleeper wears it on the arm. If he or she snores, the gadget sends a gentle signal to the brain and the snoring stops, but the person doesn't wake up.

2 Which of these gadgets would you like to buy? Why?

3 *Pair work* Think of an unusual gadget that you'd like to buy. What is it for? Where can you use it?

8 Let's celebrate!

1 SNAPSHOT

HOLIDAYS AND FESTIVALS

January or February Chinese New Year: Chinese people celebrate with firecrackers and lion dances.

May 5 Children's Day (formerly Boys' Day): Japanese families put up colored streamers shaped like fish, in honor of their children.

October 31 Halloween: American children wear costumes and go "trick or treating."

November 2 Day of the Dead: Mexican families have picnics in cemeteries and offer food to the dead.

December 25 Christmas: People in many countries decorate Christmas trees and give each other presents.

Discussion

Do you have any similar holidays in your country?

What other special days do you have?

What's your favorite holiday or festival?

2 WORD POWER

1 *Pair work* Add these words to the word map.

anniversary   cards   fireworks   presents
birthday   champagne   flowers   roast turkey
cake   dancing   parade   wedding

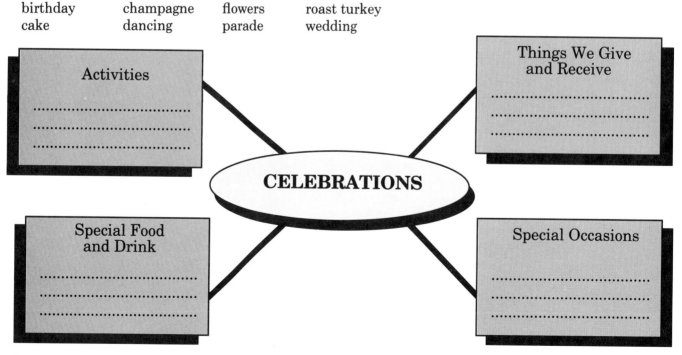

Activities
....
....
....

Things We Give and Receive
....
....
....

CELEBRATIONS

Special Food and Drink
....
....
....

Special Occasions
....
....
....

2 Now add six more words to the map. Then compare with a partner.

3 CONVERSATION 📼

Listen and practice.

A: Did you know it's St. Patrick's Day next week?
B: Oh, is it? What happens then?
A: Well, it's a day when Irish people wear green.
   And there's usually a big parade and lots of
   parties. Would you like to come to a party?
B: Sure.
A: Good! Remember to wear something green!
B: OK. Maybe I'll wear that green tie you gave me
   for my birthday!

4 GRAMMAR FOCUS: Relative clauses of time 📼

> March 17th is **the day when the Irish remember St. Patrick.**
> October is **the month when Canadians celebrate Thanksgiving.**
> August is **the month when many Europeans go on vacation.**

1 How much do you know about these special days? Complete the
sentences in column A with information in column B. Then compare
with a partner.

A

a) February is the month when
b) April Fool's Day is a day when
c) May Day is a day when
d) The Fourth of July is the day when
e) July 14th is the day when
f) New Year's Eve is a night when

B

.... Brazilians celebrate Carnival.
.... people like to party.
.... the French celebrate their revolution.
.... people play tricks on friends.
.... people in many countries honor workers.
.... Americans celebrate their independence.

2 Now complete these clauses with information of
your own.

a) Winter is a season when . . .
b) Valentine's Day is a day when . . .
c) Spring is a time of the year when . . .
d) Mother's Day is the day when . . .
e) July is a month when . . .
f) A birthday is a day when . . .
g) A wedding anniversary is a time when . . .

3 Write four more sentences like these about
special days and times. Then compare with a
partner.

5 LISTENING 📼

Mike has just returned from Jordan.
Listen to him talking about Ramadan,
a special time in the Islamic year.
Take notes.

What is Ramadan?
How long does it last?
When do people eat during Ramadan?
When does the fast begin and end?
What happens at the end of Ramadan?

6 ONCE A YEAR

1 *Pair work* Take turns asking and answering these
questions and other questions of your own.

What's the most
interesting holiday
or festival in your
country?

When is it?

How do people
celebrate it?

Do you eat any special
food?

What do you like most
about it?

What else do people do?

2 *Class activity* Give a short talk about an interesting holiday or
festival and answer any questions your classmates may have.

7 WRITING

1 What is your favorite holiday or festival? What
usually happens? What do you usually do? Make
notes and then write about it like this.

*My favorite day of the year is Christmas. Everyone
in my family gets together at my parents' house. We
sit around the Christmas tree and exchange presents.*

2 *Pair work* Read each other's compositions.
Do you have any questions?

8 CONVERSATION 📼

1 Listen and practice.

A: You look beautiful in that kimono, Mari. Is this your wedding photo?
B: Yes, it is.
A: Do most Japanese women wear kimonos when they get married?
B: Yes, many of them do. Then after the wedding ceremony, the bride usually changes into a Western bridal dress during the reception.
A: Oh, I didn't know that.

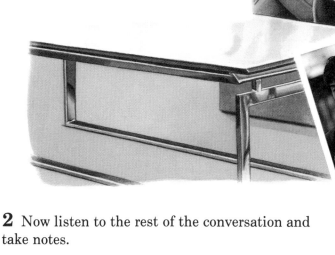

2 Now listen to the rest of the conversation and take notes.

Where was Mari's wedding held?
Who attended the wedding ceremony?
What happened at the reception?

9 PRONUNCIATION: Stress and rhythm 📼

1 The words with the most important information in a sentence are usually stressed. Listen to these sentences and then practice them.

When Jápanese wómen get márried, they úsually wéar kimónos.

After the wédding céremony, they chánge into Wéstern clóthes.

2 *Pair work* Now mark the stress in these sentences. Then listen and check, and practice the sentences.

Halloween is a time when children go trick or treating.
On Thanksgiving Day, Americans eat turkey and cranberry sauce.
When people have birthdays, they usually get presents from friends.
June is the month when many young people like to get married.

10 GRAMMAR FOCUS: Adverbial clauses of time 🔊

> **Before a Japanese couple gets married,** they send wedding announcements.
> **When they get married,** they usually wear kimonos.
> **After they return from the honeymoon,** they move into their own home.

1 Read this information about marriages in North America. Complete the clauses in column A with information in column B.

A

a) Before a man and a woman get married,
b) Before the man gets married,
c) When the woman gets engaged,
d) When the woman gets married,
e) After the couple gets married,
f) After they return from their honeymoon,

B

.... the newlyweds usually live on their own.
.... she usually wears a white wedding dress.
.... they usually date each other for a year or so.
.... his friends often give him a bachelor party.
.... her friends often give her a bridal shower.
.... there's usually a wedding reception.

2 *Pair work* What happens when people get married in your country? Complete the clauses in column A with your own information. Pay attention to rhythm and stress.

11 MARRIAGE CUSTOMS

Group work Talk about marriage customs in your country. Ask these questions and others of your own.

How old are people usually when they get married?
Is there an engagement period? How long is it?
Who pays for the wedding?
Who is invited?
Where is the wedding ceremony usually held?
What happens during the ceremony?
What do the bride and groom usually wear?
Is there a reception after the ceremony?
What type of food is served at the reception?
What kinds of gifts do people usually give?
Where do couples like to go on their honeymoon?
How long is the honeymoon?

▶ **Interchange 8: Once in a blue moon**

How do your classmates celebrate special events? Find out on page 113.

12 READING: Unusual customs

Read about these unusual customs. Then find the best title for each passage.

.... A Day for Kids
.... Choosing the Right Clothes
.... Blessing the Animals
.... Everything New for New Year's
.... Shouting "Goodbye" to Winter
.... A Special Kind of Meal

"SOMETHING OLD, SOMETHING NEW, SOMETHING BORROWED, SOMETHING BLUE..."

a) On the evening of February 3rd, people in Japanese families take one dried bean for each year of their age and throw the beans on the floor, shouting "Good luck in! Evil spirits out!" This is known as "Setsubun," a time to celebrate the end of winter and the beginning of spring.

b) Before the Chinese New Year, many Chinese families burn the picture of their kitchen god, Tsao Chen, to bring good luck. When New Year's Day comes, they put a new picture of Tsao Chen on the wall.

c) When American women get married, they sometimes follow an old custom in choosing what to wear on their wedding day. The custom says the bride must wear "something old, something new, something borrowed, and something blue." This is to bring good luck.

d) Before Lent (a time on the Christian calendar), the people of Ponti, Italy, eat an omelet made with 1,000 eggs. People cannot eat meat or dairy products during Lent, so they try to use up these things before Lent begins.

e) When winter ends in Czechoslovakia, children make a straw man called "Smrt," which is a figure of death. Then they burn it or throw it in the river. After they destroy it, they carry flowers home to show the arrival of spring.

f) January 17th is St. Anthony's Day in Mexico. It's a day when people bring their animals to church. But before the animals go into the church, the people dress them up in flowers and ribbons. This ceremony is to protect people's animals.

9 Back to the future

1 SNAPSHOT

PAST, PRESENT, AND FUTURE

People who . . .
would like to be transported
  into a past time: 30%
  into a future time: 67%
think we were better off in the past: 26%
think we will be better off in the future: 35%
would like to live to be a hundred years old: 50%
have made reservations for flights to the moon: 92,000
think they look younger than they are: 57%

Discussion
Would you like to be transported into the future? When?
Do you think people were better off in the past than now?
Will we be better off in the future?
Would you like to make a reservation for a flight to the moon?

2 CONVERSATION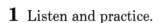

1 Listen and practice.

Cindy: Grandma, do you think people were better off in the past than they are now?

Grandma: Well, yes, in some ways, because people didn't rush around like they do today.

Cindy: Yeah, I guess so.

Grandma: But there are some things I like better today.

Cindy: Really? Like what?

Grandma: Well, I love my new car! And I couldn't live without my computer! I'm really hooked on computer games!

2 Listen to the rest of the conversation. Would Cindy prefer to live today or in a different century? Why?

3 GRAMMAR FOCUS: Time contrasts 📼

Past	**Present**	**Future**
In the past, people **didn't travel** so much.	These days, people **travel** a lot more.	Soon, people **will travel** to other planets.
Families **used to stay** home more.	Nowadays, they **don't stay** home so much.	In fifty years, workers **may work** at home.
Fifty years ago, people **lived** to around sixty.	Today, people **live** to about seventy-five.	In the future, people **may live** to a hundred.

1 Complete the phrases in column A with suitable information in column B. Then compare with a partner.

A

a) About a hundred years ago,
b) Before jet travel,
c) In most offices today,
d) In many cities around the world,
e) In the next fifty years,
f) In two hundred years,

B

.... pollution is a serious problem.
.... the world's supply of oil may run out.
.... cities began to build the first subway systems.
.... it took more than twelve hours to fly from New York to Paris.
.... there will probably be cities on the moon.
.... people work a forty-hour week.

2 *Pair work* Complete these phrases and then compare with a partner.

   Five years ago, I . . .   Now, I . . .   In five years, I'll . . .

4 PRONUNCIATION: Pitch 📼

1 Listen to how the first phrase has lower pitch than the main clause in these sentences.

In the past, people didn't travel so much.

These days, people travel a lot more.

Soon, people will travel to other planets.

2 Listen and practice the sentences you completed in Exercise 3.1.

3 Now complete the phrases in column A in Exercise 3.1 with information of your own. Then practice them with a partner. Pay attention to pitch.

5 LISTENING 📼

Listen to statements about different things. Check (✓) if the person is describing something in the past, present, or future.

	Past	*Present*	*Future*
a)			
b)			
c)			
d)			

	Past	*Present*	*Future*
e)			
f)			
g)			
h)			

6 CHANGING TIMES

Group work   Talk about how things have changed. Choose two of these topics or other topics of your own. Then discuss the questions below.

clothing   housing
education   transportation
entertainment   work
health

What was it like a hundred years ago?
What's it like today?
What will it be like in a hundred years?

7 WRITING

1 Write about your hopes for the future. (Don't put your name on your paper.)

In ten years, I'll be a successful actress. I'll be famous, and I'll star in movies and on TV...

2 *Class activity*   Pass your compositions around the class. Read another student's paper. Can you guess who wrote it?

8 CONVERSATION 🔊

Listen and practice.

A: You know, I really should give up
   smoking. I'm up to two packs a day.
B: Yeah, and it's getting more expensive,
   too. If I gave up smoking, I could save
   about $100 a month.
A: The trouble is, though, if I stop
   smoking, I'll probably gain weight.
B: Uh-huh. And if I stop, I might start
   chewing my nails again.
A: Mmm. Well, I guess I'd only stop
   smoking if they passed a law banning
   cigarettes.
B: Me too. Got a match?

"I really should give up smoking."

9 GRAMMAR FOCUS: *If*-clauses with modals 🔊

If I give up smoking, **I will** probably gain weight.
                        I might start chewing my nails again.

If they ban the sale of cigarettes, the government **may** raise taxes.

If I stopped smoking, **I could** save about $100 a month.

If they passed a law against smoking, people **would** be healthier.
                                        I'd probably quit.

1 Complete the clauses in column A with information in column B.
Then compare with a partner and practice them.

A

a) If they banned smoking on all planes,
b) If people used their cars only on
   weekends,
c) If they build a good subway system,
d) If people ate less meat,
e) If the city passes a law against keeping
   dogs as pets,

B

.... the streets will be a lot cleaner.
.... some people would travel by train.
.... they would probably be a lot healthier.
.... there would be less pollution in cities.
.... more people might get rid of their cars.

2 *Pair work* Now take turns and complete the clauses in column A
with your own information.

10 LISTENING 📼

Listen to people
complaining.
Why are they
complaining?
What laws would they
like to see passed?

Complaint   Law
a)
b)
c)

---

11 THERE SHOULD BE A LAW AGAINST IT!

1 *Group work* What are some things
that really bother you? What should be
done about them? Choose three problems
and talk about them like this.

A: I wish they'd do something about the
city parks. People leave trash all over
the place.

B: Yeah, you're right. If people leave trash
in the parks, they should pay a $500
fine.

2 Now describe a law you would like to see
passed.

If people leave trash in a public park,
they should have to work on a clean-up
crew for a weekend to clean up the park.

3 *Class activity* Compare your laws.

---

12 WORD POWER: Strong feelings

1 Look at these ways of expressing strong feelings.

People who leave trash around the parks really bother/infuriate/disgust me!

I hate/can't stand people who throw cigarette butts on the ground!

Barking dogs really make me angry/mad/disgusted!

I think the new Town Hall is awful/horrible/terrible/ridiculous!

2 Now describe five things you feel strongly about.
Then compare with a partner.

13 READING: Against the law

▶ **Interchange 9:
Pros and cons**
Join the debate! Turn to page 114 and give your opinion on some controversial topics.

1 Read this information about unusual laws.

New York City

Sark

a) Sailors are not allowed to whistle on ships at sea. This is because people used to believe that whistling would bring high winds and cause danger to the ship.

b) In seventeenth-century Japan, it was against the law for any citizen to leave the country. Anyone who was found leaving the country or arriving from overseas without permission was sentenced to death.

c) In Russia in the eighteenth century, it was against the law for any man to wear a beard unless he paid a special tax.

d) In 1949, in Illinois, U.S.A., bird lovers tried to get a law passed that would keep cats on a leash in public. However, the governor refused to pass the law. He said the problem of cats against birds is as old as time itself. If we favor birds, then we will have to decide between dogs and cats or even birds and worms.

e) In New York City, dog owners who walk their dogs in public are required by law to clean up after their pet. Before the law was passed in 1978, over forty million pounds of dog waste were left on the city's streets each year.

f) It's against the law to drive an automobile or any other motor vehicle except tractors on the island of Sark in the English Channel. Most of the people there use bicycles for transportation.

g) In Venice, Italy, many people travel through the canals on gondolas. The law requires gondolas to be painted black, except those belonging to high government officials.

2 Find nouns that mean:

- having consent to do something: .... (paragraph b)
- money collected by the government: .... (paragraph c)
- a length of rope or a chain used to control an animal: .... (paragraph d)
- an animal that lives with people: .... (paragraph e)
- something that carries things or people from one place to another: .... (paragraph f)
- people who hold an office: .... (paragraph g)

[1] What's the problem?

1 *Role play* Student A is a clerk in a repair shop.
Student B is a customer who has a problem with one of the things below.
The customer describes the problem and the clerk suggests what is
wrong.

A: Hello. Can I help you?
B: Yes, something's wrong with my . . .
A: Oh, what's the problem?
B: . . .
A: OK. Let me have a look at it.
    Perhaps . . . Yes, you see, it's the . . .
B: Oh, really?
A: Yes. Can you leave it here for repair?
B: . . . And how much will it cost?
A: Well, it should . . .
B: And how long do you need to repair it?
A: Um, I think it will take about . . . Can
    you come back on . . .?
B: . . . Thanks very much.
A: . . .

2 Now change roles and talk about another item.

[2] Listening 📼

1 Listen to some information about unusual marriage customs. Are the
statements below true (**T**) or false (**F**)?

a) When two women of a tribe in Paraguay want to marry the same
man, they put on boxing gloves and fight it out.
b) When a man and a woman get married in Malaysia, they eat some
cooked rice the day before the wedding.
c) In northeastern India before a girl gets married, she rides through the
village on a horse.
d) In some parts of India when a man and a woman get married, water
is poured over them.

2 Now listen again. For the statements you marked false, what is the
correct information?

3 That's an interesting custom!

1 *Group work* In many countries, there are interesting customs for births, marriages, the seasons, or good luck. What interesting customs do you know? Take turns talking about them like this.

When a boy courts a girl in some parts of the Philippines, he stands outside her house at night and sings to her.

Others ask questions.

Why does he do that?
Is it just a village custom?
Is it common?
Do women do the same thing?

2 *Class activity* Which was the most interesting custom you talked about in your group? Tell the class about it.

4 Classroom rules

1 *Pair work* What rules would be useful in your classroom? Think of some interesting rules for these situations.

If students . . .
    don't do their homework, they must . . .
    arrive late for class, they will have to . . .
    use their native language during class, they must . . .
    miss a class, they will have to . . .

If a student has a birthday, the class will . . .

If it's the teacher's birthday, the students will . . .

2 *Class activity* Compare your rules.

10 I don't like working overtime

1 SNAPSHOT

WORK! WORK! WORK!

Number of jobs the average worker in North America has held
  by the age of forty: 8
People who say Monday is their favorite day of the week: 3%
People who say they are at their best in the morning: 56%
Average number of hours worked each week: 1973 – 40.6; 1985 – 47.3
Workers who live within twenty minutes of work: 52%
Working wives who earn more than their husbands: 20%
Working women who say they would stay home with their children
  if they could afford it: 88%
People who say they don't have exciting jobs: 72%

Discussion
How many jobs have you had?
How long does it take you to get to work or school?
How many hours do you work or study each week?
What's your favorite day of the week? What's your worst day? Why?

2 CONVERSATION

1 Listen and practice.

A: Are there any interesting jobs in the paper today?
B: Well, here's one for a tour guide. But you have to work Saturdays and Sundays.
A: I don't want to work on weekends.
B: Neither do I. Oh, there's another here for a salesperson. It's a job selling children's books.
A: Sounds interesting.
B: Yes, but you need a driver's license, and I can't drive.
A: Oh, I can! I just got my license. What's the phone number?
B: It's 798–3455.

2 Now listen to the rest of the conversation.
What else does the job require?

3 GRAMMAR FOCUS: Statements and responses 🔊

I can type.	So can I.	I can't.
I can't use a word processor.	Neither can I.	Oh, I can!
I'm good at math.	So am I.	Gee, I'm not.
I'm not good at languages.	Neither am I.	I am!
I like office work.	So do I.	Oh, I don't!
I don't enjoy sales work.	Neither do I.	Well, I do!

1 Make responses to these statements. Then compare with a partner.

a) I don't have a driver's license.
b) I'm not very good at writing reports.
c) I can speak three languages.
d) I don't like working overtime.
e) I'm pretty good at economics.
f) I can't type very fast.
g) I like working on weekends.

2 Now write five statements like the ones above about yourself.

4 PRONUNCIATION: Stress in responses 🔊

1 Listen to the stressed words in these responses.
Then practice them.

So can **I.**   **Neither** can **I.**
So am **I.**   **Neither** am **I.**
So do **I.**   **Neither** do **I.**

2 Now listen to the stressed words in the responses to these statements.
Then practice them.

Statements	*Responses*
I don't like working on Saturdays.	Oh, **I** do!
I can't use a computer.	**I** can!
I really like studying grammar.	Gee, **I** don't.

3 *Pair work*   Take turns reading the statements you wrote in Exercise 3.2.
Pay attention to stress in your responses.

5 LISTENING 📼

Listen and choose the correct response.

a) .... So do I.
   .... So can I.

b) .... So can I.
   .... Neither do I.

c) .... So am I.
   .... So can I.

d) .... Oh, I do!
   .... Neither can I.

e) .... Oh, I can!
   .... Oh, I don't!

f) .... So am I.
   .... Oh, I don't!

6 JOB FILE

1 *Group work* What skills and job preferences do you have? Take turns asking questions like these and others of your own.

Are you good at spelling?
   math?
   writing letters?
   remembering names?

Can you type fast?
   use a computer?
   write English well?
   speak any foreign
      languages?

Do you have a driver's license?
   any office skills?
   any sales experience?
   any special diplomas or certificates?

Do you like traveling?
   sales work?
   commuting?
   a regular nine-to-five job?

A: Can you type fast, Rosa?
B: I guess so. How about you, Sam?
C: Oh, I can't! My typing is terrible! What about you, Kenji?
D: My typing is pretty bad, too.

Useful expressions

Sure.   I guess so.
So-so.   Not really.
About average. Actually, no.

2 Now think of jobs for people in your group.

A: Well, Sam, I think you should be a lifeguard.
B: Yeah, you shouldn't be a personal secretary.

▶ **Interchange 10: Nine to five**

Advertise your skills and work experience! Turn to page 115.

7 WORD POWER: Adjectives

1 Match these adjectives with definitions. Then compare with a partner.

a) easygoing   .... is very intelligent
b) forgetful   .... has good manners
c) funny   .... always keeps a promise
d) generous   .... thinks deeply about things
e) polite   .... doesn't worry about things
f) reliable   .... likes giving things to people
g) serious   .... doesn't remember things
h) shy   .... likes to be around people
i) smart   .... likes making people laugh
j) sociable   .... doesn't say much in front of
                   other people

2 Can you give definitions for these words?

bad-tempered   creative   patient   prejudiced   talkative

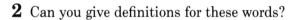

8 CONVERSATION

Listen and practice.

A: Have you met the new sales manager?
B: Yes, I have.
A: What do you think of him?
B: Well, he seems very nice. He's very friendly, and he's always helpful.
A: Oh, do you think so?
B: Yes, but I think he's kind of forgetful. He never remembers my name.
A: Yeah, you're right. He's very forgetful.
B: Oh, do you know him?
A: Yes, he's my husband!

9 LISTENING

1 Listen to four conversations about people. Do you hear something positive (**P**) or negative (**N**)? Circle the correct answer.

a) P   N   b) P   N   c) P   N   d) P   N

2 Now listen to descriptions of three other people.
Check the best adjective to describe each person.

a) .... bad-tempered   b) .... creative   c) .... unfriendly
    .... patient   .... forgetful   .... generous
    .... reliable   .... serious   .... strange

10 GRAMMAR FOCUS: Adjectives and adverbs 🔊

Adjectives	Adverbs + adjectives
He's **forgetful**.	He's **really forgetful**.
He's a **forgetful** man.	He's a **really forgetful** man.
She's **friendly**.	She's **pretty friendly**.
She's a **friendly** woman.	She's a **pretty friendly** woman.
He's not **reliable**.	She's not **very reliable**.
He's not a **reliable** person.	She's not a **very reliable** person.

1 Use the words in parentheses to complete the sentences.
Then compare with a partner.

a) My boss is pretty .... and he's .... generous. (very, easygoing)
b) My next-door neighbor is not a very .... person. He's kind of .... and .... very sociable. (not, friendly, shy)
c) My sister is .... smart and she's very .... But she's sometimes .... (creative, really, forgetful)
d) My best friend is a .... sociable person, and he's .... too. But he is very .... (funny, impatient, pretty)

2 Describe three of your classmates. Does your partner agree?

11 OPINION POLL

1 *Pair work* Choose a well-known person to describe. Give as much information as you can.

2 *Class activity* Now pairs take turns describing the person they talked about. Can anyone guess who it is?

Yo-Yo Ma

Diana,
Princess
of Wales

Julio
Iglesias

12 WRITING

1 Describe members of your family.
How similar or different are they?

I'm very different from my parents.
My father is a very serious person.
But he's very patient and...

2 *Pair work* Exchange papers and compare your families.

13 READING: You and your handwriting

Graphology is the study of handwriting. Some people believe that we can learn a lot about people's character and personality by looking at their handwriting. By studying the size, shape, width, and angle of the letters people write, we can often guess what they are like.

1 Read the list below. It shows different ways people write the letter "t" and what their handwriting says about them.

a)	*t*	confident, smart, and serious
b)	*t*	kind, polite, and patient
c)	*t*	outgoing, talkative, but impatient
d)	*t*	hardworking, but often forgetful
e)	*t*	impatient and always unreliable
f)	*t*	shy, quiet, and not very confident
g)	*t*	dreamy and sometimes shy
h)	*t t*	creative, smart, and funny
i)	*t*	proud and not very friendly
j)	*t*	emotional and careful
k)	*t t t*	outgoing and often emotional
l)	*t*	friendly and funny
m)	*t*	serious, reliable, and independent

2 *Pair work* Write the first sentence in the reading passage above. Then compare your handwriting with your partner. How are they similar or different?

3 Now compare how you wrote the letter "t" and read what your handwriting says about you. Do you agree?

11 It's really worth seeing!

1 SNAPSHOT

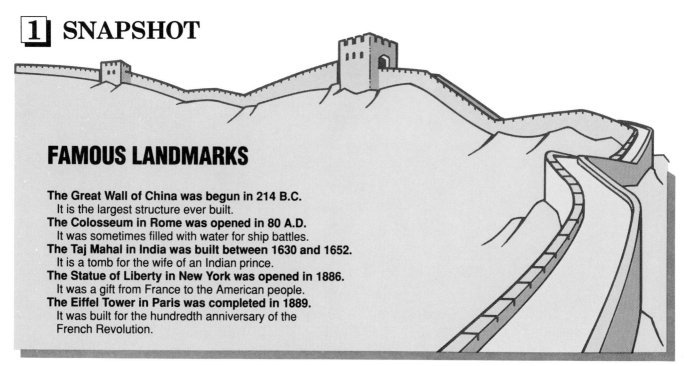

FAMOUS LANDMARKS

The Great Wall of China was begun in 214 B.C.
It is the largest structure ever built.
The Colosseum in Rome was opened in 80 A.D.
It was sometimes filled with water for ship battles.
The Taj Mahal in India was built between 1630 and 1652.
It is a tomb for the wife of an Indian prince.
The Statue of Liberty in New York was opened in 1886.
It was a gift from France to the American people.
The Eiffel Tower in Paris was completed in 1889.
It was built for the hundredth anniversary of the
French Revolution.

Discussion
Do you know anything else about these landmarks?
What are the five most famous landmarks in your city?

2 CONVERSATION 📼

1 Listen and practice.

A: Have you studied for the test tomorrow?
B: Yes, I have.
A: OK. Let me quiz you on the Panama Canal.
B: All right. Go ahead.
A: Who was the canal built by?
B: It was started by the French and completed by the Americans.
A: Right! And when was it completed?
B: It was completed in 1911.
A: No! It was completed in 1914.
B: Oh, that's right.

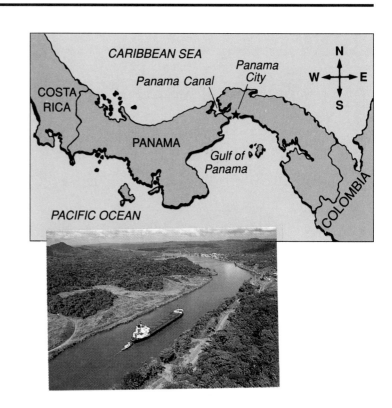

2 Now listen to the rest of the conversation.
How long is the canal?
How long does it take to go through it?
How many ships go through it every year?

3 WORD POWER: Connections

1 The list below contains four kinds of landmarks. Arrange the words into four groups. Then compare with a partner.

a) art gallery
b) bridge
c) canal
d) church
e) memorial
f) monument
g) museum
h) observatory
i) shrine
j) statue
k) temple
l) tunnel

2 *Pair work* How many more words can you add to each group?

4 GRAMMAR FOCUS: The passive with *by* 🔳

Active	Passive
The French **started** the Panama Canal.	The Panama Canal **was started by** the French.
The Romans **built** the Colosseum and the Forum.	The Colosseum and the Forum **were built by** the Romans.

1 Complete the phrases in column A with suitable information in column B. Then compare with a partner.

A

a) The novel *1984*
b) The pyramids
c) The Statue of Liberty
d) The mural in the Sistine Chapel in Vatican City
e) The novel *Gone With the Wind*

B

.... was designed by Bartholdi.
.... was written by George Orwell.
.... were built by the ancient Egyptians.
.... was written by Margaret Mitchell.
.... was painted by Michelangelo.

2 Now change these active sentences into passive sentences with **by.** Then compare with a partner.

a) Leonardo da Vinci painted the *Mona Lisa.*
b) Marie Curie discovered radium.
c) Mildred and Patty Hill wrote the song "Happy Birthday to You."
d) Mark Twain wrote the American novel *Huckleberry Finn.*
e) Thomas Edison invented the phonograph and the light bulb.

5 PRONUNCIATION: Linked sounds 📼

1 Final consonants are often linked to the vowels that follow them. Listen and practice.

Montreal is one of the biggest cities in Canada.
The Colosseum in Rome was opened in 80 A.D.
Thomas Edison is famous for a lot of inventions.

2 Now mark the linked sounds in these sentences. Listen and check, and then practice them. Pay attention to the linked sounds.

The Suez Canal in Egypt is over eighty kilometers long.
The Museum of Modern Art is a famous art museum in New York.

6 BRAIN TEASERS

1 *Pair work* Think of six questions about famous buildings, landmarks, paintings, books, or musical compositions.

Who was <u>Starry Night</u> painted by?
Who was <u>Don Quixote</u> written by?
Who was <u>Madame Butterfly</u> composed by?

2 *Group work* Take turns asking your questions. Who got the most correct answers?

7 LISTENING 📼

1 Listen to a tour guide describing some famous buildings and landmarks in Washington, D.C. Take notes and then answer the questions below.

a) *The Jefferson Memorial*

Who was Thomas Jefferson?
When was the memorial completed?

b) *The Washington Monument*

How high is the monument?
When was it opened?

c) *The White House*

How many rooms does it have?
Who was it designed by?

2 *Pair work* Take turns asking the questions.

8 CONVERSATION 📼

Listen and practice.

A: Hello?
B: Oh, hello. I need some information.
   What currency is used in Japan?
A: Where?
B: In Japan.
A: I'm not sure. Isn't it the yen?
B: Oh, yes. And do they drive on the left or
   the right?
A: I think the left, but I'm not sure.
B: Oh. Well, is English spoken much
   there?
A: I really have no idea.
B: Uh? Well, what about credit cards? Are
   American Express cards used there?
A: How would I know?
B: Well, you're a travel agent, aren't you?
A: What? A travel agent? This is Linda's
   Hair Salon.
B: Oh, sorry, wrong number!

9 GRAMMAR FOCUS: The passive without *by* 📼

Active	Passive
They **use** the yen in Japan.	The yen **is used** in Japan.
They **speak** both Spanish and Portuguese in Latin America.	Both Spanish and Portuguese **are spoken** in Latin America.
They **export** a lot of rice here.	A lot of rice **is exported** here.

1 Complete these sentences using the passive and suitable verbs below.

eat   grow   make up   manufacture   speak   teach   wear

a) Both cars and computers .... in Korea.
b) English .... in grade school in Singapore.
c) A great deal of cotton .... in Egypt.
d) Frogs and snails .... in France.
e) Canada .... of ten provinces and two territories.
f) Kimonos .... sometimes .... in Japan.
g) French .... not widely .... in Great Britain.

2 Now use the verbs above and write sentences like these about your
country. Use the passive. Then compare with a partner.

10 WHAT DO YOU KNOW?

1 *Pair work*   How many of these questions can you answer?
(Answers are on page 134.)

a) Where is Algeria located?
b) What languages are spoken in Belgium?
c) Where is most of the world's rubber produced?
d) How many countries can you name where English is spoken as a second language?
e) Can you name four countries where French is spoken?
f) Can you name three countries that are governed by a prime minister?

2 Now write three more world-knowledge questions like these. Then ask
them around the class.

11 LISTENING 🔲

1 Listen to a teacher giving a talk about Guatemala.

Where is Guatemala located?
What countries are located on its borders?
How big is Guatemala?
What is its population?

2 Now listen to the rest of the talk and fill in the chart.

Guatemala

Capital city:_____
Average income:_____
Religions:_____
Languages:_____
Industries:_____
_____
Export crops:_____
_____

▶ **Interchange 11:
Culture quiz**

What instrument did Liberace play?
Who was the song "Material Girl"
sung by? Group A turn to page 116
and Group B to page 118.

12 READING: Amazing Brazil

1 How much do you know about Brazil? Circle the answers below.

a) Brazil is the (2nd, 5th, 10th) largest country in the world.
b) It is located in the (northern, eastern, western) part of South America.
c) The capital city is (Rio de Janeiro, Brasília, São Paulo).
d) The official language is (Spanish, English, Portuguese).
e) Brazil has a population of around (38, 138, 500) million.
f) Brazil is the world's largest producer of (coffee, oil, cotton).

2 Now read this information. Then check your answers by underlining the correct information in the passage.

Brazil, the largest country in South America and the fifth largest country in the world, is located in the eastern half of South America. The people of Brazil are famous for their outgoing, friendly, and fun-loving nature. They love to sing, dance the samba, and sunbathe. And on the beach, both men and women wear the briefest bikinis! Brazilian women are considered to be among the best dressed in the world.

Brazil is a federal republic with 23 states. The capital city is Brasília. Portuguese is the official language, and it is spoken with a distinct Brazilian accent. Brazil has a population of over 138 million, which is made up of people of many different races and ethnic groups. People of Portuguese and African descent and of mixed blood make up the vast majority. In addition, there are immigrants from Germany, Italy, Japan, and many other countries. Eighty percent of the population is Roman Catholic.

A number of industrial products are manufactured in Brazil,

including cars, chemicals, ships, machines, and military weapons. Mining is also an important industry, and Brazil is the world's second largest exporter of iron ore. Precious stones and metals, such as emeralds and gold, are also mined. Agriculture is another important industry. Many crops are exported, including coffee (Brazil is the largest grower in the world), cotton, soybeans, sugar, cocoa, rice, corn, and fruit.

13 WRITING

1 Write a short composition about a country. Include information about location, population, and other topics, as above.

2 *Pair work* Exchange compositions and answer any questions.

12 It's been a long time!

1 CONVERSATION 📼

1 Listen and practice.

A: Hey, Joan! I haven't seen you since graduation!

B: Yeah, it's been a long time, Pete!

A: So, what have you been doing since then?

B: Well, right after I graduated, I married the boy next door. But, unfortunately, it didn't work out. Now I'm back at school. How about you?

2 Listen to the rest of the conversation.
What did Pete do after he graduated?

2 WORD POWER: Verbs

1 Arrange these verbs into the lists below. Then compare with other students.

| ✓commute | divorce | graduate | marry | separate | teach |
| date | drive | major | move | study | walk |

Travel
commute

Relationships

School

2 Now choose four of the verbs and use them in sentences.

I used to drive to work, but now I take the subway.

74

3 GRAMMAR FOCUS: Past tense, past continuous, and present perfect continuous 📼

Past tense	Past continuous	Present perfect continuous
I **graduated** three years ago.	I **was studying** in Britain in 1989.	I **have been working** since 1988.
I **got** married in January.	I **was living** with my parents before that.	We **have been living** in California for two years.

Complete these sentences using a suitable tense and the verbs given. More than one correct answer may be possible. Then compare with a partner.

a) Two years ago, I .... (stay) in a dormitory.
b) I first .... (start) learning English in 1990.
c) At this time last year, I .... (work) in a bank.
d) I .... (take) English classes here for the past six months.
e) My family .... (live) in the same house for ten years.
f) I .... (go) to primary school in Ottawa and high school in Vancouver.
g) My sister .... (get married) in Australia.
h) I .... (live) in Puerto Rico before I moved here.
i) I .... (jog) every day for over a year.

4 LISTENING 📼

Listen to people talking at a party and choose the correct response.

a) .... For a year.
    .... A year ago.

b) .... Yes, I was.
    .... Yes, I have.

c) .... For ten years.
    .... In ten years.

d) .... For two years.
    .... In 1990.

e) .... Five years ago.
    .... For five years.

f) .... In 1987.
    .... Since 1987.

5 REALLY? HOW INTERESTING!

1 *Pair work* How similar are you and your partner? Take turns
asking some of these questions and others of your own.

Did you go to school here?
        grow up here?

How long have you been studying English?
                wearing glasses?
                going to this school?

Have you been living in this city all your life?
        married for long?

What were you doing last summer?
                this time last year?
                two years ago?

Where did you study English before you came here?
        meet your wife/husband?

Useful expressions

How about you?	Is that so?	Oh, really?
Me, too.	How interesting!	

2 *Class activity* Tell the class the most interesting thing you
learned about your partner.

---

6 SNAPSHOT

BEFORE AND AFTER

Jobs some celebrities once did

Clint Eastwood: gas station attendant
Whoopi Goldberg: high school teacher
Cyndi Lauper: waitress
Bette Midler: worker in a pineapple factory in Hawaii
Arnold Schwarzenegger: manager of a body-building club

Original names of some celebrities

Norma Jean Baker (Marilyn Monroe)
Reginald Dwight (Elton John)
Maurice Micklewhite (Michael Caine)
Charles Buchinski (Charles Bronson)
Annie Mae Bullock (Tina Turner)

Whoopi Goldberg

Arnold Schwarzenegger

Discussion

Do you know any other celebrities who had regular jobs before they became famous?
Why do you think celebrities sometimes change their names?
If you became a celebrity and had to choose a new name, what name would you choose?

7 CONVERSATION 📼

1 Listen and practice.

A: So tell me a little more about yourself, Sharon.
B: Well, when I graduated from drama school, I tried to get a job as an actress in Hollywood.
A: Really?
B: Yeah, but I didn't get any parts. After two years, I finally got a job with Universal Studios.
A: So you finally got to be an actress?
B: No, I'm a tour guide at the studio! But while I'm on the job, I get to see a lot of stars!

2 Now listen to the rest of the conversation. What did Ed do after he graduated? What does he do now?

8 GRAMMAR FOCUS: Adverbials 📼

Adverbial clauses

Before I moved here, I lived in Germany.
When I was a student, I studied drama.
While I was at school, I worked part-time.
After I graduated, I tried to get a job.

Adverbial phrases

During school vacations, I used to sell cosmetics.
After graduation, I traveled around Europe.
Before 1989, I worked as a tour guide.

1 Match the clauses and phrases in column A with suitable information in column B. More than one answer is possible. Then compare with a partner.

A

a) During my childhood,
b) While I was in grade school,
c) When I was twelve,
d) After I left high school,
e) Before 1988,
f) Before I started taking this English course,
g) After my last vacation,

B

.... I won a diving competition at school.
.... I was broke.
.... I studied English with a Canadian friend.
.... I didn't have a job.
.... I lived with my grandparents.
.... I traveled in southeast Asia.
.... my parents moved to the U.S.

2 Now complete the clauses and phrases in column A with information of your own. Then compare with a partner.

9 PRONUNCIATION: Sentence stress 📼

1 Notice the stressed words in these sentences.

When I was a **stu**dent, I studied **dra**ma.

After gradu**a**tion, I **tra**veled around **Eu**rope.

2 Now listen and practice the sentences in Exercise 8.1.

10 HIDDEN SECRETS

Class activity Go around the class and try to find people who did the following things. Stop after five minutes. How many names do you have?

Did you . . .   *Names*

a) have an unusual pet during your childhood?
b) pass your driver's test the first time?
c) use to read comic books during class in high school?
d) have your first date before you were fifteen?
e) try smoking cigarettes before you graduated from high school?

11 LISTENING 📼

1 *Group work* How much do you know about these people?

a)

b)

c)

Who are they? Where were they born?
What did they do before they became famous?
What are some of the important things they did during their lives?
What do people remember them for?

2 Now listen to information about each person and take notes.

3 *Pair work* Take turns. Choose one of the people and use your notes to talk about his or her life.

12 READING

1 Read this passage. Can you think of a good title for it?

HOANG NHU TRAN is a former Vietnamese refugee who was recently chosen as one of America's twenty outstanding college students. When he graduated from the U.S. Air Force Academy, he was accepted by Harvard Medical School. His life is a remarkable story of his escape from war-torn Vietnam to success in the United States.

Hoang was born in Saigon in 1966 and spent the early part of his childhood there. When Saigon fell in 1975, Hoang and his family escaped on a boat with two hundred other people. They sailed for three days, and then they were picked up by a rescue ship and taken to Guam. They stayed there for a month. After that, they went to California as refugees. Later, they settled in a trailer park in Fort Collins, Colorado, and Hoang started school.

While he was at school, Hoang studied hard and was an outstanding student. After he graduated from high school, he won a full four-year college scholarship. However, he chose instead to enter the U.S. Air Force Academy. With a double major in biology and chemistry, Hoang made the dean's list six times.

He also became the school's wrestling champion, played on the rugby team, and was an expert marksman.

And what are Hoang's plans for the future? He says, "Maybe I'll be in aviation medicine, maybe an astronaut. But at the end, I want to serve the world, to help all mankind."

2 *Pair work* Cover the passage. How many things can you remember about Hoang Nhu Tran?

3 How do you explain the success of people like Hoang Nhu Tran?

13 WRITING

1 Write a short biography of an interesting person in your family (e.g., a grandparent, an aunt or uncle) or of a celebrity.

My grandmother came to Canada in 1924. She was born in Poland. She came to Canada when she was seven. Her first job was in a store. I'll always remember my grandmother because...

▶ **Interchange 12:
Rolling Stone reporter**

Would you enjoy reporting on the rich and famous? Student A turn to page 117 and Student B to page 119.

2 *Pair work* Exchange papers and answer any questions your partner may have.

Review of Units 10–12

1 Me, too!

Group work One student makes a statement about one of the following things.

something you . . . are good at doing or not good at doing
can do well or can't do well
like or don't like
enjoy doing or don't enjoy doing
hate doing

Then the student points to someone else in the group. That student responds and makes another statement, like this.

A: I hate doing housework. *(points to someone)*
B: So do I!
  I can't whistle. *(points to someone else)*
C: Neither can I.

Useful responses
So/Neither am I.
So/Neither can I.
So/Neither do I.

2 My kind of person

1 *Group work* What do you think are the three most important qualities for (a) a friend and (b) a wife or husband?
Choose these adjectives or use adjectives of your own.

| easygoing | generous | independent | smart | sociable |
| funny | hardworking | patient | serious | reliable |

Talk about them like this: I think a friend should be . . .
It's important for a husband to be . . .

2 *Class activity* Compare your choices.

3 I know that!

1 *Group work* Write down ten statements about countries, places, famous buildings or landmarks, etc. Five should be true and five false.

Spanish is spoken in Chile.   (T)
Car tires are usually made of plastic. (F) (rubber)

2 *Class activity* Take turns. One group reads its statements and another group answers. Which group gets the most correct answers?

4 Listening 📼

Listen to people on a TV game show answer questions about Spain.
What are the answers? Take notes.

a) currency
b) driving
c) population
d) capital
e) popular sport
f) neighboring countries

5 Test your memory!

Pair work   Take turns asking these questions.

What were you doing . . .

four hours ago?
at nine o'clock last night?
at this time yesterday?

What were you wearing . . .

yesterday?
the day before yesterday?
three days ago?

6 School days

Pair work   Talk about your school
days and ask questions like these.

> Where did you go to school?
> Who was your favorite teacher?
>   Why?
> What subjects did you study while
>   you were in high school?
> What was your best subject?
> What was your worst subject?
> Who was your best friend?
> Did you belong to any clubs when
>   you were in school?
> What did you usually do during
>   school vacations?
> What do you remember most about
>   your school days?

13 A terrible book, but a terrific movie!

1 SNAPSHOT

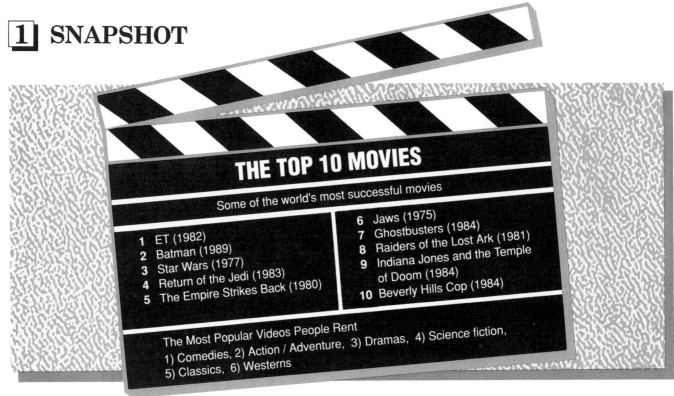

THE TOP 10 MOVIES

Some of the world's most successful movies

1 ET (1982)
2 Batman (1989)
3 Star Wars (1977)
4 Return of the Jedi (1983)
5 The Empire Strikes Back (1980)

6 Jaws (1975)
7 Ghostbusters (1984)
8 Raiders of the Lost Ark (1981)
9 Indiana Jones and the Temple of Doom (1984)
10 Beverly Hills Cop (1984)

The Most Popular Videos People Rent

1) Comedies, 2) Action / Adventure, 3) Dramas, 4) Science fiction, 5) Classics, 6) Westerns.

Discussion
How many of the movies above have you seen?
Which one is your favorite?
What are the three best movies you have seen in the past year?
What kinds of videos do you watch?

2 CONVERSATION 📼

1 Listen and practice.

James Dean

A: Are you interested in a movie tonight?
B: Um, maybe. What's on?
A: There's a new Dirty Harry movie playing.
B: Oh, I can't stand Clint Eastwood! He's so boring. All he does is stand around and try to look macho.
A: Oh, come on! Well, then, how about a James Dean movie? They're showing *Rebel Without a Cause* at Cinema City.
B: Now that sounds interesting! I've never seen it, and I really like James Dean.

2 Now listen to the rest of the conversation.
What happened next? What did they decide to do?

3 GRAMMAR FOCUS: Participles 🔊

Past participles	**Present participles**
I'm **interested** in old movies.	Old movies are **interesting**.
I was **bored** by the book.	The book was **boring**.
I was **surprised** by how the movie ended.	The ending of the movie was **surprising**.

1 Complete these sentences with the past or present participle of the words in parentheses.

a) I'm not .... in horror movies. (interest)
b) I find nature films .... (fascinate)
c) I'm .... with watching television. (bore)
d) I didn't like *Batman* at all. I was ....
that it was so successful. (surprise)
e) *Star Wars* was a pretty .... movie. (excite)
f) Meryl Streep is a very .... actress. (interest)
g) I'm .... by Stephen King's novels.
(fascinate)
h) I thought *The Russia House* was a ....
book. (bore)
i) It's .... they don't make many
westerns these days. (surprise)

2 Now write six sentences like the ones above about movies, actors, actresses, or novels. Use your own information. Then compare with a partner. Does your partner agree?

4 LET'S GO TO THE MOVIES!

1 *Pair work* Take turns asking these questions and others of your own.

How often do you go to the movies?
What kinds of movies are you interested in?
What kinds of movies don't you like? Why?
Do you have a favorite actor?
Who's your favorite actress?

What's one of the best movies you have ever seen?
What did you like about it?
What are your three favorite movies in English?
Are there any interesting movies on now?

2 *Group work* Compare your information.

5 PRONUNCIATION: Word stress 📼

1 Mark if these words are stressed on the first or second syllable. Then listen and check, and practice them.

favorite	ridiculous	surprising	terrific
interesting	successful	terrible	unusual

2 Now listen and practice these sentences. Pay attention to word stress.

ET is my favorite movie.
I thought *Ghostbusters 2* was ridiculous!
Robert de Niro is a terrific actor.

6 WORD POWER: Adjectives

1 Put these words on the word map below.

boring	dumb	odd	silly	terrific	weird
disgusting	fascinating	ridiculous	terrible	unusual	wonderful

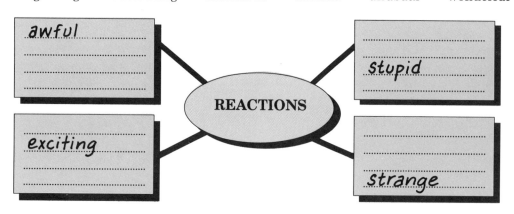

awful

exciting

REACTIONS

stupid

strange

2 Now look at these words. Do they describe a positive (+) or a negative (−) reaction?

dreadful	fantastic	marvelous	pathetic
excellent	horrible	outstanding	

3 *Pair work* Use some of the adjectives above to describe movies, actors, and actresses. Pay attention to word stress.

7 LISTENING 📼

Listen to people talking about books and movies. Check (✓) the best adjective to describe what they say about each one.

a) .... fascinating .... silly .... strange
b) .... wonderful .... odd .... boring
c) .... boring .... terrific .... dreadful
d) .... ridiculous .... interesting .... exciting

A terrible book, but a terrific movie!

8 CONVERSATION 🔊

Listen and practice.

A: Oh, I've never read this. What's it about?

B: It's a horror story. It's about a guy who goes crazy and tries to kill his family.

A: Is it any good?

B: Not really. It's too long. The movie was a lot better. Jack Nicholson's in it, and he's really terrific. Hey – why don't you just rent the video?

A: Good idea! Would you like to come over and see it?

B: Yeah, sure. I'll bring some popcorn.

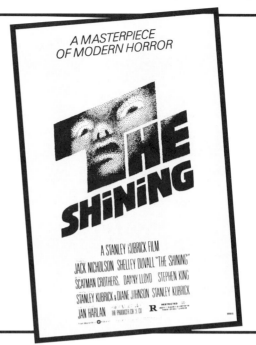

9 GRAMMAR FOCUS: Relative clauses 🔊

Use *who* or *that* for people	Use *which* or *that* for things
It's about a guy. He tries to kill his family.	It's a comedy. It stars Eddie Murphy.
It's about a guy **who/that** tries to kill his family.	It's a comedy **which/that** stars Eddie Murphy.

1 Join these sentences with **who, that,** or **which.** Then compare with a partner.

a) *West Side Story* is a musical. It has some wonderful songs in it.

b) Leonard Bernstein is the composer. He wrote the music for *West Side Story.*

c) Marilyn Monroe was the actress. She starred in *Some Like It Hot.*

d) *War and Peace* is a book. It is really fascinating.

e) *Ran* is a wonderful film. It's about life in medieval Japan.

f) The movie *2001* is about two astronauts. They are on a fatal mission.

g) Stephen Spielberg is a director. He has made many successful films.

h) *ET* is a science fiction movie. It has made over $200 million.

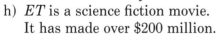

85

2 *Pair work* Complete these sentences with relative clauses.

a) Sean Connery is an actor who . . .
b) *Jaws* is a movie that . . .
c) Marilyn Monroe was an actress who . . .
d) Walt Disney was a famous movie director who . . .
e) *Batman* is a movie that . . .
f) Michael Jackson is a singer that . . .
g) Sophia Loren is an actress who . . .

10 SCRIPT WRITERS

1 *Group work* You are script
writers for a television studio. You
have to write a new script for a TV
detective show. Think of an
interesting story.

> Where does the story take place?
> Who are the main characters?
> What are the main events?
> How does the story end?

© BBC

2 *Class activity* Now tell the class about your story.

> Our story is about a bank robbery that takes place in Chicago.
> There are three main characters . . .

11 LISTENING 📼

1 Listen to two critics talking about a new movie.
What do they like or not like about it? Mark the
chart like this:

3 = liked it very much
2 = OK
1 = didn't like it

	Pauline	Colin
Acting	....	....
Story	....	....
Photography	....	....
Special effects	....	....

2 How many stars do
you think each critic
gave the movie?

★★★★ excellent ★★ fair
★★★ very good ★ poor

3 Now listen to the critics give their ratings.

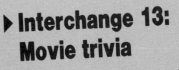

▶ **Interchange 13:
Movie trivia**

Are you crazy about movies?
Turn to page 120.

12 READING: Movie reviews

1 Read these movie critics' reviews of *The Last Emperor*. How do you think each critic rated the film?

★★★★ excellent   ★★ fair
★★★ very good   ★ poor

Movie Director's Last Epic

In *The Last Emperor*, director Bernardo Bertolucci not only gives us a fascinating history lesson but also a compelling human drama. It is the story of Pu Yi, who came to the throne in 1908 at the age of 2. The performances are outstanding, and the movie is spectacular in every way. The 3 hours fly by, and the audience leaves feeling they have gotten to know a great country and a sensitive, unusual man.

The Emperor's New Clothes

Don't go see *The Last Emperor* if you're expecting a history lesson. Bertolucci's epic about the rise and fall of Pu Yi is hard to follow and confusing at times. But he has done a remarkable job of portraying the Chinese culture, and he has captured China in stunningly beautiful images. There are some touching scenes, as when the young Pu Yi's nurse is taken from him. Unfortunately, the movie is too long and tends to drag at times.

What a Drag!

Bernardo Bertolucci is a talented director. Why he made *The Last Emperor* is a mystery. True, the scenery and costumes are nice. But the main character is passive and dull – he simply watches his life go by. You'd expect a film which covers 60 years of history to be exciting. But the 3 hours of *The Last Emperor* drag on forever. At least the film is consistent – consistently boring.

2 *Pair work* Which words in each review helped you decide on the critics' ratings?

13 WRITING

1 *Pair work* Choose a movie you have both seen recently and discuss it. Then write a review of it.

What was the movie like?
Did you enjoy it?
What did you like or not like about it?
How would you rate it?

2 *Class activity* Now exchange reviews. Do you agree?

14 Say what you mean!

1 SNAPSHOT

LANGUAGES

Number of languages in the world: *about 4,000*
Languages with the greatest number of native speakers:
  Chinese, English, Spanish, Hindi, Arabic, Bengali, Russian,
  Portuguese, Japanese, German
Number of English words in *Webster's Third New International Dictionary*: *450,000*
Number of English words added to Japanese since 1945: *about 20,000*
Some words in English from other languages: *alcohol, cotton (Arabic); ketchup,*
  tea (Chinese); judo, karate, kimono (Japanese); cafeteria, tornado (Spanish)

Discussion

Can you name some countries where these
  languages are spoken: Arabic, Portuguese, and
  Spanish?
What are ten common words in your language that
  come from other languages?

2 CONVERSATION 📼

1 Listen and practice.

A: I'm glad we rented this car. Now we can get
  around and see the sights!
B: Yeah. You know, these highways are really
  great, but the road signs are pretty confusing.
A: Mmm. What do these lines on the road mean?
B: They may mean you can't pass here.
A: Well, I'm going to pass anyway – I want to go
  around this car. It's going too slow.
A: Now, I wonder what this sign means.
B: I think it means you have to turn left in this
  lane.
A: Yeah, or maybe it means you can turn left if
  you want to. I think I'll just go straight.

2 Now listen to the rest of the conversation.
Which picture shows the highway they were
driving on?
Which sign is the police officer talking about?

3 GRAMMAR FOCUS: Modals and adverbs 📼

> This sign **may** mean you **can** pass here.
> That **might** mean you **have to** turn right.
> It **could** mean you **must** turn left there.
>
> It **probably** means there's no passing.
> **Perhaps** it means you **can't** pass here.
> **Maybe** that means you **can** make a U-turn.

Drawing by S. Harris;
© 1988 The New Yorker Magazine, Inc.

1 What do you think these signs mean? Make sentences as in the grammar box, choosing suitable phrases from below. Then compare with a partner.

This sign may mean . . .

- there's a steep hill ahead
- this parking space is for the handicapped
- this area is reserved for wheelchairs
- you should stop if other traffic is approaching
- there's a pedestrian crossing ahead
- the road is slippery when it's wet
- there's road construction ahead
- you should watch out for falling rocks
- you can't make a U-turn here

a)

b)

c)

d)

e)

f)

g)

2 *Pair work* Now talk about these signs.
What do you think they mean?

4 WORD POWER: Definitions

1 Match each word with a definition. Then compare with a partner.

A: What does . . . mean?
B: It means . . .

a) confident (adj.)   .... a saying people use in conversation
b) controversial (adj.)   .... causing strong disagreement or argument
c) diligent (adj.)   .... a reason someone gives for doing or not doing something
d) excuse (n.)   .... confused
e) puzzled (adj.)   .... sure about something
f) proverb (n.)   .... to remember
g) recall (v.)   .... to change something from one language into another
h) translate (v.)   .... hardworking

2 *Pair work*   Can you give definitions for these words?

apologize (v.)   criticize (v.)   idiom (n.)
arrogant (adj.)   divorced (adj.)   slang (n.)

5 PROVERBS

1 *Group work*   Here are some common proverbs in English. What do you think they mean?

A penny saved is a penny earned.
A stitch in time saves nine.
Don't burn your bridges behind
   you.
Every cloud has a silver lining.
One person's meat is another
   one's poison.

Talk about them like this:

I think it means . . .   Well, it could mean . . .
Or perhaps it means . . .   It probably means . . .

2 Now think of some interesting proverbs from your own language and write them down in English. What do they mean?

3 *Class activity*   Tell the class about one of the proverbs you discussed.

6 LISTENING 📼

1 Listen to Albert inviting friends to his birthday party. What excuses do people give for not coming? Draw a line from each person to the excuse he or she gives.

1. Scott
2. Fumiko
3. Manuel
4. Regina

She said that she wasn't feeling well.
He said he was taking his mother to a disco.
She said she had house guests for the weekend.
He said that he would be out of town.
She said she might go out with a friend.
He said he was going away with his family.

2 Now it's the night of Albert's birthday party. Listen. What happened?

7 GRAMMAR FOCUS: Reported speech 📼

Statement	Reported speech
I **am** not **feeling** well.	She said (that) she **was** not **feeling** well.
I **am taking** my mother out.	He said he **was taking** his mother out.
I **have made** other plans.	. . . said she **had made** other plans.
I **didn't get** the invitation.	he **hadn't gotten** the invitation.
I **can't come**.	she **couldn't come**.
I **will be** out of town.	he **would be** out of town.
I **may go** ice skating.	she **might go** ice skating.
There **is** an office party.	there **was** an office party.

Look at these excuses. Change them into reported speech and then compare with a partner.

Cindy: "There is a party on Friday at my parents' house."

Cindy said there was a party on Friday at her parents' house.

a) Bob: "I am leaving town for the weekend."
b) Mary: "I have been invited to a wedding on Saturday."
c) Jim: "I promised to help Joanne move."
d) Ann: "I can't come because I have the flu."
e) John: "I will be studying for a test all weekend."
f) Susan: "I have to meet someone at the airport."

8 NEVER ON SUNDAY!

1 Your teacher wants to have an extra class on Sunday afternoon. You don't want to go. Make up an excuse.

I'm taking my dog to the hairdresser.

2 *Class activity* Talk to three classmates. What excuses do they give?

A: Are you coming to the class on Sunday?
B: No. I have an appointment with my masseur.

3 Now tell the class the best excuse you heard.

Jack said he was taking his grandmother to a wrestling match.
Sue said that she had a belly dancing lesson.

9 LISTENING AND WRITING 📼

Nancy is out of town for the weekend. Listen to four messages on her answering machine. Her roommate has written down the first one. Write down the other messages.

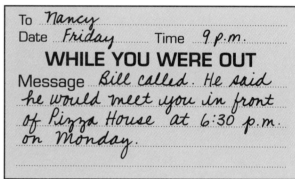

To *Nancy*
Date *Friday*   Time *9 p.m.*
WHILE YOU WERE OUT
Message *Bill called. He said he would meet you in front of Pizza House at 6:30 p.m. on Monday.*

10 PRONUNCIATION: Information focus 📼

1 If we want to emphasize one piece of information in a sentence, we give it extra stress. Listen to these examples.

A: John said he'd meet you at the library on **Friday.**
B: Oh, I thought he said **Thursday.**

A: John said he'd meet you at the **library** on Friday.
B: Oh, I thought he said the **cafeteria.**

2 Listen to these short conversations between two people. Underline the word that the first speaker is emphasizing.

a) Terry said there was a baseball game at the stadium on Saturday.

b) Maria said Joe and Betty are getting married on Sunday.

c) Dean said he couldn't come to school tomorrow.

d) Liz said there was a message for you in the office.

3 *Pair work* Now take turns reading the sentences above in different ways to emphasize different information.

11 READING: The truth about lying

Do you ever give excuses that are not really true? When and why?

It seems that everybody tells lies – well, not big lies, but what we call "white lies." The only real questions are about when we lie and who we tell lies to. A recent study found that in conversation people frequently stretch the truth. Here are some ways they do it.

#1 Lying to hide something: People often lie because they want to hide something from someone. For example, a son doesn't tell his parents that he is dating a girl because he doesn't think they will like her. Instead, he says he is going out with the guys.

#2 Giving false excuses: Sometimes people lie because they don't want to do something. For example, someone invites you to a party. You think it will be boring so you say that you are busy and can't come.

#3 Lying to make someone feel good: Often we stretch the truth to make someone feel good. For example, your friend cooks dinner for you, but it tastes terrible. Do you say so? No! You probably say, "Mmm, this is delicious!"

#4 Lying to hide bad news: Other times we don't want to tell someone bad news. For example, you have just had a very bad day at work, but you don't want to talk about it. So, if someone asks about your day, you just say everything was fine.

Telling white lies isn't really all bad. Most of the time people do it because they want to protect a friendship.

1 Do you know any other reasons people tell white lies?

2 *Pair work* Now look at these situations. Are they examples of #1, #2, #3, or #4? More than one answer is possible.

a) You borrowed a friend's motorcycle and scratched it. You are having it painted. The friend wants the motorcycle back. You say the engine didn't sound right and you are having it checked.

b) Your friend gives you an ugly vase for your birthday. You say, "Oh! It's beautiful!"

c) Someone you don't like invites you to a movie, so you say, "I've already seen it."

d) You're planning a surprise party for a friend. To get her to come over at the right time, you ask her to stop by to see your new video player.

▶ **Interchange 14: Who said that?**
What makes your classmates mad? Turn to page 121 for answers to this and other intriguing questions.

15 What would you do?

1 SNAPSHOT

WHAT A FORTUNE!

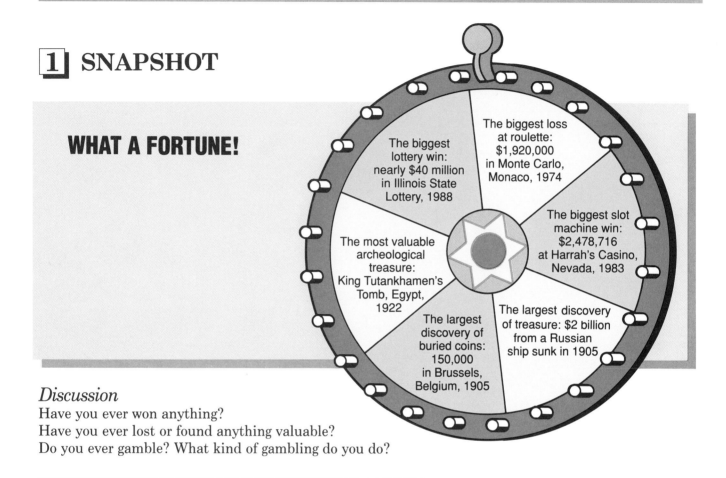

The biggest lottery win: nearly $40 million in Illinois State Lottery, 1988

The biggest loss at roulette: $1,920,000 in Monte Carlo, Monaco, 1974

The biggest slot machine win: $2,478,716 at Harrah's Casino, Nevada, 1983

The most valuable archeological treasure: King Tutankhamen's Tomb, Egypt, 1922

The largest discovery of treasure: $2 billion from a Russian ship sunk in 1905

The largest discovery of buried coins: 150,000 in Brussels, Belgium, 1905

Discussion
Have you ever won anything?
Have you ever lost or found anything valuable?
Do you ever gamble? What kind of gambling do you do?

2 CONVERSATION 📼

Listen and practice.

A: Look at this! Someone just won $10 million in the lottery! How come I never choose a winning number?

B: Well, what would you do if you won $10 million?

A: Me? Well, first I'd quit my boring job at the bank. And then I'd buy a boat and sail around the world!

B: That's all? I'd go straight to Monte Carlo and try my luck in the casinos. I bet I could turn it into *$20* million!

A: Yeah, and *I* bet you could lose it all in a day!

3 GRAMMAR FOCUS: *If*-clauses with *would* and *might* 🔲

> What **would** you do **if you won $10 million?**
>
> **If I won $10 million,** I **would** sail around the world.
> I **might** quit my job.
> I'**d** probably faint.
> I **wouldn't** spend it all at once.

1 Complete the clauses in column A with suitable information in column B. Then compare with a partner.

A

a) If I found a burglar in my home,
b) If I saw someone shoplifting,
c) If I found a lot of money,
d) If the teacher gave me an A by mistake on a test,
e) If I locked myself out of my house,
f) If I didn't like a meal I got in a restaurant,

B

.... I'd break a window to get in.
.... I'd run to my neighbors for help.
.... I might not tell anybody.
.... I'd probably call the police.
.... I guess I might spend it.
.... I wouldn't pay for it.
.... I might tell a salesclerk.
.... I'd point out the error.

2 Now complete the clauses in column A with your own information. Then compare with a partner.

3 *Pair work* Now think of three more situations like the ones above. Then ask another pair of students what they would do.

4 PREDICAMENTS

1 *Group work* What would you do in the situations below?

A: What would you do if . . . ?
B: I think I'd . . .
C: I'm not sure, but I might . . .

- you found a valuable piece of jewelry on a park bench
- you won a lot of money in a lottery
- a friend borrowed money from you and didn't return it
- you were on vacation overseas and lost all your money and credit cards
- you saw two people fighting on the street
- you discovered your friend has a drinking problem
- someone stole your clothes on the beach while you were swimming

2 *Class activity* Choose three of the best suggestions and tell the class about them.

5 LISTENING 🔘

1 Listen to three people talking about three different predicaments.
What are they? Write them in the chart below.

2 Now listen again. What do you think the best suggestion was for each
predicament? Complete the chart and then compare answers around the
class.

Predicament	*Best suggestion*
a)	
b)	
c)	

6 WORD POWER: Verbs

1 Find nine pairs of opposites in this list. Then compare with a partner.

accept	borrow	dislike	find	marry	return
admit	deny	divorce	forget	refuse	save
agree	disagree	enjoy	lose	remember	spend

2 *Pair work* Now choose four pairs of opposites and use each pair in
a sentence.

I can never save money because I spend it all on clothes.

7 CONVERSATION 📼

1 Listen and practice.

A: Hi! Is your house guest still staying with you?

B: No, after three weeks, she finally left. Thank goodness!

A: So how did you get rid of her?

B: Well, I lied and told her my parents were coming for a visit and I needed the room. I feel bad about it, though. What would you have done?

A: Oh, I would have told her to leave after a week. By the way, my father-in-law is coming to visit us next week. Can I move in with you for a few days?

B: No way!

2 If this happened to you, what would you do?

8 PRONUNCIATION: Reduced form of *have* 📼

1 Listen to the reduced form of **have** in these sentences.

What would you **have** done?

I would **have** told her to leave.

2 Now practice these sentences. Use the reduced form of **have.**

You could have said something.
You should have told me.

You might have asked me about it.
You shouldn't have said anything.

9 GRAMMAR FOCUS: Past modals 📼

What **would** you **have done?** I **would have told** her to leave.
I **wouldn't have done** anything.
I **would have asked** her about it.

What **should** I **have done?** You **could have spoken** to her about it.
You **shouldn't have made** her leave.

1 Read the situations in column A. What do you think would have been the best thing to do? Choose suitable suggestions from column B and then compare with a partner.

A

a) My aunt gave me a cigarette lighter for my birthday. But I don't smoke.
b) I saw a classmate cheating on an exam. So I wrote her a letter about it.
c) A friend of mine often smells bad. So I put some deodorant in his bag.
d) I hit someone's car as I was leaving a parking lot. Luckily no one saw me.
e) The teacher borrowed my favorite book and spilled coffee all over it.

B

.... You should have spoken to him about it.
.... I would have told her that I'd prefer something else.
.... I would have spoken to the teacher about it.
.... I would have waited for the owner to come back.
.... You could have exchanged it for something else.
.... I wouldn't have said anything.
.... You could have warned her not to do it again.
.... You could have left a note for the owner.

2 *Pair work* Now give another suggestion for each situation. Use the reduced form of **have**. Then compare answers around the class.

10 SECOND CHANCES

1 Think about things that have happened in your life during the last few years. What opportunities did you miss? Write down five things you should or shouldn't have done like this.

I should have married my first girlfriend.
I shouldn't have voted for...

2 *Group work* Now talk about your missed opportunities.

11 LISTENING 🔲

1 Listen to people calling Dr. Hilda, a counselor on a radio talk show. Take notes.

What happened to each caller?
What did they do?
What should they have done?

2 Do you agree with Dr. Hilda? What would you have done?

▶ **Interchange 15: What would you have done?**

Sometimes there are no right answers! Turn to page 122 and see what *you* would have done in these difficult situations.

12 READING: Miss Manners

Read these letters to Miss Manners' advice column and find the most suitable reply to each one.

Dear Miss Manners,

I was invited to a dinner party recently. I thought it would be okay to dress casually, so I wore jeans and a sweater. When I got there, all the guests were dressed up and I felt really awkward. Should I have gone home and changed my clothes?

Underdressed

Dear Miss Manners,

Someone told me my brother's wife was seeing another man. The next time I saw her, I spoke to her about it, but she denied it. Recently, I found out the rumor wasn't true. Now my sister-in-law won't speak to me.

Ms. Busybody

Dear Miss Manners,

I was at a friend's house for dinner recently. During dinner I accidentally broke a beautiful vase. It was my friend's favorite wedding present. I offered to pay for it, but she refused. I still feel bad about it.

Feeling Guilty

Dear ....

I think you did the right thing. These things sometimes happen. But perhaps you could give her a special gift to make up for it.

Miss Manners

Dear ....

It depends on how well you know the hostess. If she was a good friend, you could have apologized and explained your misunderstanding. If you didn't know her well, it would have been better to excuse yourself and return later in something more suitable.

Miss Manners

Dear ....

Well, you learned a lesson. You shouldn't have listened to gossip. Now you have to repair the damage. The best thing to do is to apologize sincerely and hope that she will forgive and forget.

Miss Manners

Dear ....

You should have thought more carefully before you acted as you did. It really wasn't necessary to get angry. The best thing to do in situations like that is to speak to the child immediately and warn him or her not to do it again.

Miss Manners

13 WRITING

1 *Pair work* Write a letter to Miss Manners about an awkward situation or a problem like the ones in Exercise 12.

2 *Class activity* Put your letters on the bulletin board. Then choose one and write a reply to it.

Review of Units 13–15

1 Critics' choice

1 *Group work* What are the three best movies you have seen recently?

2 Why do you think these three movies are the best? Talk about the
things below and then rank the movies from 1 to 3 (1 = best).

the story   the photography   the special effects
the acting   the music   why you liked it so much

3 *Class activity* Now report on your three favorite movies to the class.

2 Leisure time

1 *Group work* What are your favorite leisure time activities? Ask
these questions and talk about what you do in your free time.

How many hours of TV do you watch every day?
What kinds of TV programs do you like?
What do you think are the most interesting TV shows these days?

Are you interested in sports?   What hobbies are you interested in?
How often do you play sports?   Do you collect anything?
What kinds of sports do you play?   Do you belong to any clubs?
Who are your favorite athletes?
                                       Are you interested in reading?
Are you interested in music?   What kinds of books and magazines do you like to read?
What kinds of music do you like?

2 *Class activity* Now compare your information. What are the class favorites?

3 Listening 📼

1 Listen to people talking. What are they talking about? Take notes.

a) ....   b) ....   c) ....   d) ....

2 Now listen again. What does each person mean? Check (✓) the correct response.

a) .... She is confused.   c) .... He couldn't understand it.
   .... She is afraid.   .... He thought it was very interesting.

b) .... She enjoyed it.   d) .... She thought it was all right.
   .... She hated it.   .... She thought it was terrible.

4 Good intentions

1 *Pair work*   What are some things you would like to do in the near future? Think of three good intentions.

A: I'm going to try to give up smoking.
B: I want to learn how to sail this summer.

2 *Class activity*   Now go around the class and talk to three classmates and compare your intentions. Then report the best intentions you heard.

Bob said he was going to try to lose 20 pounds.
Debbie said she's planning to get married in Hawaii in June.

5 What's the joke?

1 *Pair work*   Look at these cartoons.

What do they mean?
Do you think they are funny?
Why or why not?

"A ticket to wherever you're sending my luggage."

2 *Class activity*   Compare your reactions to the cartoons.

"I can hear the sea."

6 That sounds fantastic!

1 Think of what you would do in these situations.

a) If I had $1,000 to spend, I would . . .
b) If I could invite anyone I wanted to dinner, . . .
c) If I could take a vacation anywhere in the world, . . .
d) If I could change one thing in the world, . . .
e) If I could be a famous movie star, . . .

2 *Group work*   Now compare your answers.

Interchange Activities

Class profile

1 *Class activity* Find out which of your classmates have done the things below. When someone answers "Yes," write down his or her name. Then ask another person the next question.

Did you use to have long hair?

Did you have a cat when you were a child?

Were you born more than 500 miles away from here?

Find someone who . . .

Names

a) used to have long hair ....

b) had a cat when he or she was a child ....

c) was born more than 500 miles away from here ....

d) used to go jogging when he or she was a teenager ....

e) went to primary school and high school in his or her hometown ....

f) played soccer in school ....

g) used to collect stamps ....

h) had a part-time job in high school ....

i) used to play the piano ....

j) married someone from his or her hometown ....

2 *Pair work* Now compare your information.

Interchange 2 | Excuse me, I'm lost! – STUDENT A

1 Ask your partner how to get to the places below. Then mark them on your map.

the tourist office   the parking lot   the laundromat
the department store   McDonald's   the gas station

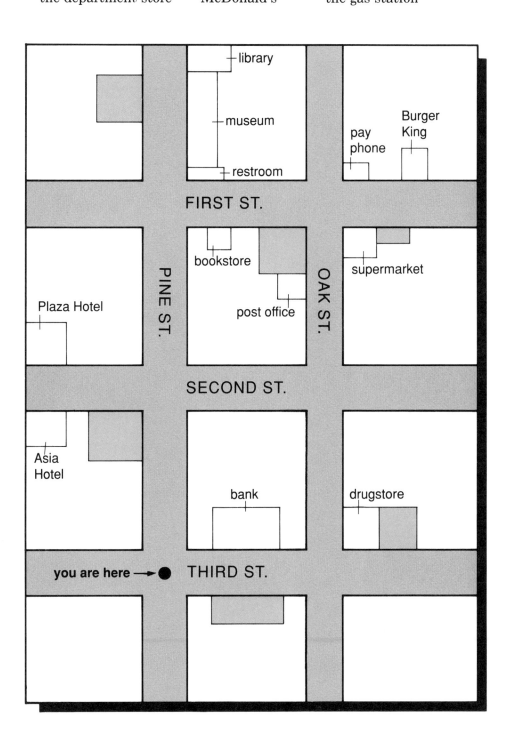

2 Now use your map and give your partner the information she or he asks for.

Interchange 2 | Excuse me, I'm lost! – STUDENT B

1 Use your map and give your partner the information she or he asks for.

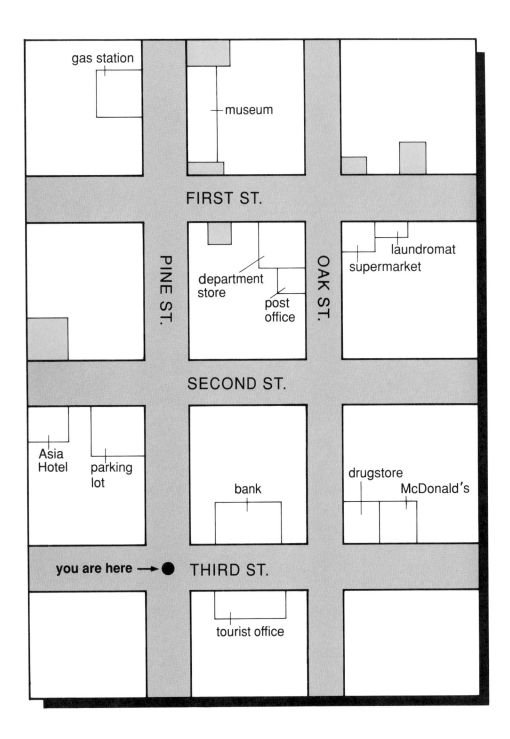

2 Now ask your partner how to get to the places below. Then mark them on your map.

the Plaza Hotel	the library	the restroom
the bookstore	Burger King	the pay phone

Interchange 3 | Housing survey

1 *Pair work* Take turns. Use the questionnaire below and find out about your partner's home and neighborhood.

a) What kind of home do you live in?
[ ] apartment   [ ] house
[ ] other _____

b) How long have you been living there?   since _____ (month / year)

c) How far from school is it?   about _____ (distance / time)

d) How big is it?   about _____ (square feet / meters)

e) How many rooms does it have? _____ rooms total

f) Does it have ...?
[ ] air conditioning   [ ] a microwave
[ ] central heating   [ ] a dryer
[ ] a dishwasher   [ ] a view
[ ] a washing machine   [ ] a pool

g) Are there any ... in your neighborhood?
[ ] restaurants   [ ] shops
[ ] supermarkets   [ ] parks
[ ] movie theaters   [ ] schools
[ ] recreation facilities

h) Is your neighborhood ...?
[ ] crowded   [ ] clean
[ ] safe   [ ] quiet

2 *Class activity* Now use the questionnaire and report your information to the class.

How many students . . .?

- live in apartments?
- live in houses?
- live close to school?
- live more than five miles from school?
- live more than twenty miles from school?
- have recreation facilities in their neighborhoods?
- live in quiet neighborhoods?

Interchange 4   Risky business

1 *Class activity*   How much do you really know about your classmates? Look at these lists and add two more things to ask in each list. Then go around the class and ask questions. Write down the names of classmates who answer "Yes" for Part (a) and "No" for Part (b).

Have you ever smoked a cigar?
Have you ever been for a moonlight swim?

Names

a) Find two people who have . . .

smoked a cigar   ....

been for a moonlight swim   ....

cried during a movie   ....

studied all night for an exam   ....

lied about their age   ....

....

....

b) Find two people who have never . . .

eaten a hot dog   ....

been on a blind date   ....

seen a wild animal   ....

kissed someone in public   ....

had a massage   ....

....

....

2 Whose names appear most on each list?

Interchange 5   Coastal fling — STUDENT A

1 *Role play*   You are at a travel agency reading about these trips to
the United States, but you are not sure which one is better for you.

This is your chance to see the U.S.

Choose a coast and have the vacation of your life!
Prices from $1,200 (not including airfare).

21-DAY EAST COAST TOUR
See three historic cities in the U.S.!
Special winter rates. Deluxe hotel
accommodations. Fantastic boat tour
available.

15-DAY WEST COAST TOUR
Visit three exciting cities! Tour available
year round. Single or double rooms.
Special harbor cruise.

Talk to the travel agent and get more information. Start like this.

> I'm going to take a trip to the U.S. Can you tell me about these tours?
>
> Which cities will I visit on the East Coast/West Coast Tour?
> What kinds of things can I do in . . . (name of city)?
> I'm going in winter/summer. What's the weather like then?
> I want to have a single/double room. How much does it cost?
> What else can I see on the East Coast/West Coast Tour?

Then tell the travel agent which tour you are going to take and why.

2 Now change roles and partners. Look at page 108.

Interchange 5 | Coastal fling — STUDENT B

1 *Role play* You are a travel agent. A customer is asking you questions about these two trips to the United States. Use the information below to answer her or his questions.

15-day West Coast Tour

Cities	Things to see and do:
San Francisco	Visit Chinatown, take a special harbor cruise (dinner served), tour the wine country in the Napa Valley
Los Angeles	Go to Disneyland, visit Universal Studios, take a tour of the movie stars' homes
San Diego	Visit the San Diego Zoo, go windsurfing or sailing
Weather:	Cool in winter and warm (hot in L.A.) in summer
Tour cost:	Single room $1,200; double room $1,500

21-day East Coast Tour

Cities	Things to see and do:
Boston	See Harvard University, visit monuments to the American Revolution, try lobster
New York	Visit the Empire State Building, see a show on Broadway, take a boat tour (stops at the Statue of Liberty)
Washington, D.C.	Take a tour of the White House, go to the National Gallery, visit the Smithsonian Museum
Weather:	Cold in winter, hot and humid in summer
Tour cost:	Single room $1,600 winter and $1,900 summer; double room $2,100 winter and $2,350 summer

Then ask the customer if there is anything else she or he wants to do there. Finally, ask which tour she or he is going to take.

2 Now change roles and partners. Look at page 107.

Interchange 6 | That's no excuse! – STUDENT A

1 *Role play*   Read each situation below and then make a complaint to your partner. Use your own words and use your imagination! Your partner will give excuses.

a) Your friend borrowed your favorite record album two weeks ago. You'd like to have it back.

b) Your friend promised to meet you at the movie theater last night. You waited in front of the Cinerama Theater, but your friend never showed up. Finally, you went in and saw the movie alone.

2 Change partners. Now it's your turn to give excuses to your partner's complaints.

a) Your neighbor is complaining about your dog. Apologize and promise you'll try to keep "Bonzo" quiet and inside the house at night.

b) Your roommate is complaining that her/his box of chocolates is empty. Explain that two friends came over and ate all of the chocolates. You couldn't stop them. Apologize and offer to buy your roommate a new box tomorrow.

Interchange 6 | That's no excuse! – STUDENT B

1 *Role play* Read each situation below. Listen to your partner's complaints and then apologize and give an excuse. Use your own words and use your imagination!

a) You borrowed your friend's favorite record album two weeks ago. You want to return it, but you can't find it. Apologize and promise to look for it tonight and to return it as soon as possible.

b) You promised to meet your friend at the movie theater last night. Your friend complains that you didn't show up at the Cinerama Theater. Apologize and explain that you thought both of you were going to the Varsity Theater. You waited at the Varsity for an hour before going home.

2 Change partners. Now it's your turn to make complaints about these situations.

a) Your neighbor has a large dog. The dog barks all night and keeps you awake. It also comes into your yard and chases your cat.

b) You got a big box of your favorite chocolates for your birthday. When you return home from school, there are no chocolates left in the box. You are sure your roommate ate all of them.

Interchange 7 | But it's almost new! – STUDENT A

1 *Role play* You are a salesclerk. A customer comes in. The customer has a problem with a video camera.

You start. Begin like this:

"Yes, may I help you?"

- Ask if the customer has checked the batteries.

- Give another suggestion for the problem (e.g., the switches need to be repaired; the whole camera needs checking).

- Ask the customer to leave the camera with you.

- Arrange a day and time when the customer can pick it up.

2 You work in a store. A customer brings back something he or she has bought. There is a problem with it.

- Suggest what the problem might be.

- Say that it needs to be repaired (or give another suitable explanation).

- Ask the customer to leave the item with you. Say when it can be picked up.

3 This time imagine you have bought something recently, but now you have a problem with it. Take it back to the store and say what is wrong with it. The clerk will give you suggestions.

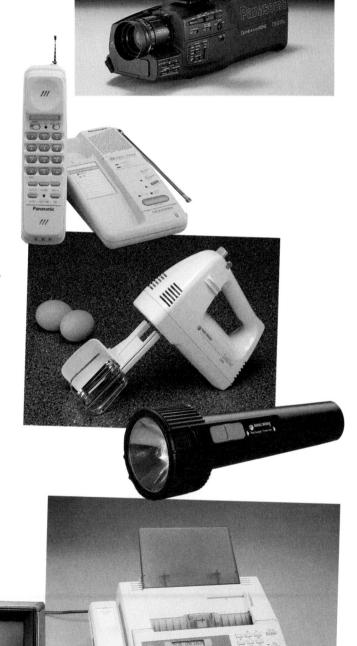

Interchange 7 | But it's almost new! – STUDENT B

1 *Role play* You bought a video camera recently, but it doesn't work. You take it back to the store. Your partner starts.

- Explain the problem.

- You have already checked the batteries. They are OK.

- The salesclerk suggests what is wrong. Agree with the salesclerk.

- The salesclerk will ask you to leave the camera for repair. You agree.

- Arrange a convenient day and time to pick it up.

2 Imagine you have bought something recently, but now you have a problem with it. Take it back to the store and say what is wrong with it. The clerk will give you suggestions.

3 This time you work in a store. A customer brings back something he or she has bought. There is a problem with it.

- Suggest what the problem might be.

- Say that it needs to be repaired (or give another suitable explanation).

- Ask the customer to leave the item with you. Say when it can be picked up.

Interchange 8 Once in a blue moon

1 *Class activity* How do your classmates and the teacher celebrate special days and times? Go around the class and ask the questions below. If someone answers "Yes," write down his or her name and ask for more information.

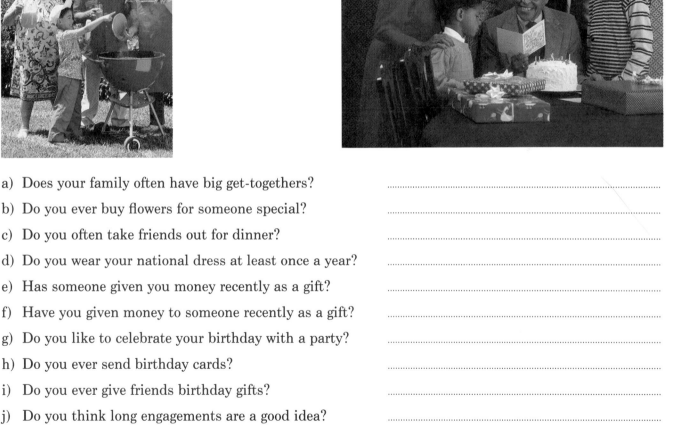

a) Does your family often have big get-togethers? ....

b) Do you ever buy flowers for someone special? ....

c) Do you often take friends out for dinner? ....

d) Do you wear your national dress at least once a year? ....

e) Has someone given you money recently as a gift? ....

f) Have you given money to someone recently as a gift? ....

g) Do you like to celebrate your birthday with a party? ....

h) Do you ever send birthday cards? ....

i) Do you ever give friends birthday gifts? ....

j) Do you think long engagements are a good idea? ....

k) Do you drink champagne at special events? ....

l) Is New Year's your favorite time of the year? ....

m) Do you ever celebrate a holiday with fireworks? ....

2 *Pair work* Now compare your information.

Interchange 9 Pros and cons

1 Read these questions about controversial suggestions and add three more of your own. Then find out some of your classmates' opinions. Ask each question to two students and check (✓) "pro" or "con."

A: Do you think it is a good idea to triple the price of cigarettes? Why or why not?

B: Yes, because people won't want to smoke anymore.

C: No, because smokers already pay enough taxes.

D: Well, if they triple the price, . . .

Do you think it is a good idea to . . . ? Why or why not?	Pro	Con
a) triple the price of cigarettes		
b) reduce the working week to four days for all workers		
c) allow people to use their cars only two days a week		
d) require fifty percent of all government employees to be women		
e) ban the sale of all products made of fur		
f) make cars that don't go faster than fifty miles (eighty kilometers) an hour		
g) require everyone to give one day a month to community service		
h) require bicycle riders to wear helmets		
i)		
j)		
k)		

2 *Class activity* How many students responded "pro" and "con" to each question?

Interchange 10 | Nine to five

1 Write one or two sentences about yourself by describing

a) your work experience;

b) something you are good at doing and not so good at;
   or

c) the kind of work you like doing and don't like doing.

The teacher will collect the information and put it on a class chart like this.

Who is this?

Name

1) I worked for five years as the manager of a bowling alley. Now I own a coffee shop called "The Jazz Cafe."

_____

2) I think I'm pretty good at making money and spending it, too. But I'm terrible at saving it!

_____

3) I hate office work like typing and photocopying. But I love working outdoors with children!

_____

2 *Class activity* Now try to find each student who wrote information on the chart. Ask questions like these.

Did you work for five years as the manager of a bowling alley?
(or) Do you own a coffee shop called "The Jazz Cafe"?

Are you pretty good at making money and spending it, too?
(or) Do you have trouble saving money?

When you find the correct person, write his or her name on the chart. Stop after ten minutes. How many names do you have?

Interchange 11 | Culture quiz – GROUP A

1 Look at these questions and then add two more questions of your own to each category.

#1 Music

a) Who was the song "Somewhere Over the Rainbow" (from *The Wizard of Oz*) made famous by? (Judy Garland)
b) What instrument did Louis Armstrong play? (trumpet)
c)
d)

#2 Movies

a) Who was the movie *ET* directed by? (Steven Spielberg)
b) What Swedish actress starred in the old movies *Camille* and *Ninotchka?* (Greta Garbo)
c)
d)

#3 Literature

a) Who was the play *Hamlet* written by? (Shakespeare)
b) Who was the book *Frankenstein* written by? (Mary Shelley)
c)
d)

#4 Art

a) Who was the impressionist picture called *Sunflowers* painted by? (Van Gogh)
b) Who was the statue *David* made by? (Michelangelo)
c)
d)

2 Now take turns asking your questions to Group B. Which group got more correct answers?

Interchange 12 *Rolling Stone* reporter – STUDENT A

1 *Role play*   Imagine you are Michael J. Fox, the famous actor. You are going to be interviewed by a reporter from *Rolling Stone* magazine. Use the information below to help you answer some of the reporter's questions about your life. Make up answers of your own if necessary.

Michael J. Fox

- born in Edmonton, Canada, on June 9, 1961
- father is a retired police officer
- mother is a payroll clerk
- moved to Vancouver at age 5
- studied drama in high school and acted in several plays
- in 1978, worked in a Canadian TV comedy series
- dropped out of high school in 1979
- when 19, moved to Los Angeles
- acted in some films
- in 1982, got a lead role in the TV series *Family Ties*
- made several successful films:
  Back to the Future (1985)
  Secret of My Success (1987)
  Bright Lights, Big City (1988)
  Casualties of War (1989)
  Back to the Future Part II (1989)
  Back to the Future Part III (1990)

2   Now change partners and roles. You are a reporter from *Rolling Stone* magazine. You are going to interview the famous rock star Cyndi Lauper. Ask the following questions and some questions of your own.

When were you born?
What did your parents do?
When did you begin singing?
Where did you go to high school?
What did you do after that?

When was *Blue Angel* recorded?
What was your first solo album?
Did you make a video of any of your hit songs?
What have you been doing recently?

Interchange 11   Culture quiz – GROUP B

1 Look at these questions and then add two more questions of your own to each category.

#1 Music

a) Who was the song "Material Girl" sung by?   (Madonna)
b) What instrument did Liberace play?   (piano)
c)
d)

#2 Movies

a) Who was the movie *Star Wars* directed by?   (George Lucas)
b) What actress is as famous for her marriage to Richard Burton as she is for her roles in movies like *Cleopatra?*   (Elizabeth Taylor)
c)
d)

#3 Literature

a) Who was the mystery *Murder on the Orient Express* written by?   (Agatha Christie)
b) Who was *On the Origin of Species* written by?   (Charles Darwin)
c)
d)

#4 Art

a) Who was Mickey Mouse created by?   (Walt Disney)
b) Who was the most famous Spanish painter of the twentieth century?   (Picasso)
c)
d)

2 Now take turns asking your questions to Group A. Which group got more correct answers?

Interchange 12 | *Rolling Stone* reporter – STUDENT B

1 *Role play* Imagine you are a reporter from *Rolling Stone* magazine. You are going to interview the famous actor Michael J. Fox. Ask the following questions and some questions of your own.

Where were you born?

What do your parents do?

Where did you grow up?

Did you study acting in school?

What did you do after that?

When did you move to Los Angeles?

Did you make any films in Hollywood before *Family Ties?*

Which movie do you like the best?

What else have you been doing recently?

2 Now change partners and roles. Imagine you are Cyndi Lauper, the famous rock star. You are going to be interviewed by a reporter from *Rolling Stone* magazine. Use the information below to help you answer some of the reporter's questions about your life. Make up answers of your own if necessary.

Cyndi Lauper

born on June 20, 1953, in New York City

parents divorced; mother worked as a waitress

began to sing and play guitar at age 12

went to several high schools

■ dropped out of high school at age 17,
but later graduated

worked as an office clerk

traveled to Canada and studied art for one year

■ returned to New York and formed a
band called "Blue Angel"

recorded the album *Blue Angel* in 1980

first solo album in 1983: *She's So Unusual*

made a video of "Girls Just Want to Have Fun" and
"Time After Time" in 1983

■ named Billboard's Top Female Album Artist in 1984

■ recorded the album *True Colors* in 1984

■ in the last few years has given concerts worldwide,
made music videos, and started film career

Interchange 13 | Movie trivia

1 *Group work* Take turns asking the questions below about movies. Then compare your answers around the class. (Answers on page 134.)

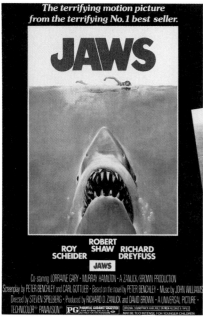

a) What famous movie was about a huge shark?

b) Can you name two movies that Dustin Hoffman was in?

c) Which famous actor is Joanne Woodward married to?

d) Can you name a movie star who is also a singer?

e) Can you name two movies directed by Alfred Hitchcock?

f) Can you name any of the actors who played the classic roles of *Dracula* and *Frankenstein?*

g) Name an actor who has played the part of James Bond.

h) Who was the actress who starred with Humphrey Bogart in *Casablanca?*

i) Can you name a movie that Eddie Murphy acted in?

j) There's a famous movie about a gorilla that climbed the Empire State Building. What's it called?

2 *Group work* Now make up your own "Movie Trivia" quiz with ten questions like the ones above.

3 *Class activity* Groups take turns asking their questions. The student who has the most correct answers is the winner.

Interchange 14 | **Who said that?**

1 *Class activity* Go around the class and ask these questions, and fill in the chart.

	Name	*Answer*
a) What's your favorite day of the year?		
b) What day of the week do you hate the most?		
c) If you could change your job, what would you be?		
d) What's the household chore you dislike doing the most?		
e) What's something other people do that really makes you mad?		
f) If you could change one thing in the world today, what would it be?		
g) What is something you would really like to get as a gift?		
h) If you could live anywhere in the world, where would you live?		
i) What is the best thing that has happened to you in the last month?		
j) If you could marry a movie star, who would it be?		

2 *Pair work* Now compare the answers you got.

A: Emilio said that his favorite day of the year was . . .
B: Well, Mai said her favorite day was . . .

Interchange 15 | What would you have done?

1 Look at the situations below. What would you have done? Circle a, b, or c.

1. A clerk in a store gave you $20 extra change by mistake.
   a. Return the money.
   b. Say nothing and keep it.
   c. Give the money to charity.

2. Another student cheated on an exam.
   a. Do nothing.
   b. Tell the teacher.
   c. Talk to the student.

3. A friend painted a picture. You thought it was awful.
   a. Say something nice about it.
   b. Say you don't like it.
   c. Say nothing.

4. You were a guest in a home. Your host offered you food that you hate.
   a. Say, "I'm not hungry."
   b. Eat the food.
   c. Say, "I don't care for that food."

2 Now interview your classmates. What do they say? Do you agree? Start like this:

A: What would you have done for number 1?

B: Well, I probably would have . . .

3 *Pair work*   Read this predicament.

Tina and Rob were just finishing dinner on Saturday when the doorbell rang. It was their good friends Cindy and Chris. They thought they had been invited to a dinner party, but they had made a mistake. The dinner party was for next week.

If you had been Tina and Rob, what would you have done? Tell your partner.

4 *Pair work*   Now make up your own predicaments. Then get in pairs. Tell your partner your predicaments, and ask what she or he would have done.

Unit Summaries

1 A time to remember

Grammar

1. Past tense questions: BE

Was I	...?	Where was I	...?
Were you	...?	Where were you	...?
Was she	...?	Where was she	...?
Was he	...?	Where was he	...?
Was it	...?	Where was it	...?
Were you	...?	Where were you	...?
Were we	...?	Where were we	...?
Were they	...?	Where were they	...?

2. Questions and statements with USED TO

Did you **use to** collect stamps?

Yes, I **used to** collect stamps.
Yes, I **did.**

No, I **didn't use to** collect stamps.
No, I **didn't.**
No, I **never used to** collect stamps.
No, I **never did.**

3. For past tense of irregular verbs, see page 133.

Key Vocabulary

Nouns
apartment
backyard
best friend
child
childhood
college
first/last name
football
foreign language
French
fun
game
high school
hobby
job
language
law student
memory
movie
Portuguese
primary school
reporter
school
singer
soccer
Spanish
sports
stamps
summer
treehouse
university
vacation
video

Verbs
be
build
buy
collect
come
do
forget
get
give
go
graduate
grow up
have
live
lose
love
major
move
play
remind
see
sell
send
sit
speak
stand
start
study
take
used to
win

Adjectives
favorite
great
part-time

Adverbs
after
anymore
as
here
just
really
there

Prepositions
for
from
in
into
to

Conjunctions
and
but
or

Other words
any
born

Titles
Mr.
Mrs.
Ms.

Wh-words
what
when
where

Expressions
Hi.
Hello.
Good morning/afternoon/evening.
We haven't met.
Could you tell me a little about yourself?
What do you want to know?

I'd like to introduce ...
I'd like you to meet ...
Nice to meet you.
Good to meet you, too.

Say, ...
Can I give you a hand?
Thanks.
Why don't you come over for coffee later?
I'd love to.
How about you?
Me, too.
Really?
Sure.
What do you do?
What should I call you in class?
Please call me ...

2 I'm just passing through

Grammar

1. Wh-questions and indirect questions: singular and plural.

> Where **is** the **shop?**
> Where **are** the **shops?**
>
> Could you tell me where the **shop is?**
> Could you tell me where the **shops are?**
>
> How often **does** the **bus come?**
> How often **do** the **buses come?**
>
> Can you tell me how often the **bus comes?**
> **buses come?**

2. For past tense of irregular verbs, see page 133.

Key Vocabulary

Nouns
airport
arts
bank
bar
block
bridge
building
bus
bus station
bus stop
city hall
coffee shop
department store
drycleaner's
entertainment center
government
Immigration Department
ma'am
main post office
market
National Gallery
number
office
officer
parking lot
restaurant
restroom
science museum
shopping plaza
sign
signal
street
subway entrance
subway station
supermarket
taxi stand
traffic light
train station
transportation

Verbs
catch
close
cost
cross
find
know
leave
look for
miss
open
say
tell
try
turn

Modal verbs
can
could

Adjectives
commercial
good
last
little
lost
nearest

Adverbs
about
after that
around here
down
far
finally
first
left
next
past
right
then
up

Prepositions
across
behind
beside
down
in back of
in front of
in the middle of
near
next to
on
on the corner of
opposite
up

Directions
north
east
south
west

Other words
another one
one
some
there's

Time expressions
an hour
quarter of an hour
half an hour
three quarters of an hour
forty-five minutes

Wh-words
how much
how often
what time
when
where

Expressions
Excuse me.
Oh, no!
Just one more thing.
Oh!
Thanks a lot.
Well, . . .
Not really.
I'm just passing through.
OK.
All right.
You're welcome.
Let me tell you how to get there.

3 That's outrageous!

Grammar

Comparisons

> **Questions with WHICH**
> Which is more interesting, Tokyo or Paris?
> Which is bigger, Toronto or Chicago?
>
> **Irregular adjectives**
> The weather is **good.**
>   **not as good as** Hawaii.
>   **better** in Hawaii.
>
> Transportation is **bad.**
>   **not as bad as** Los Angeles.
>   **worse** in Los Angeles.

For a list of comparative forms of adjectives, see page 133.

Key Vocabulary

Nouns
area
bathroom
bedroom
carpet
city
closet
coffee table
cost of living
country
couch
cupboard
downtown
entertainment
food
house
housing
kitchen
hometown
hotel
living room
neighborhood
nightlife
people
place
problem
rent
shopping
shower
sightseeing
sink
size
summer
transportation
view
weather
winter

Verbs
need
pay
show

Wh-word
which

Adjectives
all right
big
cheap
clean
cold
comfortable
cool
crowded
dangerous
dirty
exciting
expensive
friendly
hot
interesting
large
lovely
modern
nice
old
pleasant
polluted
reasonable
safe
small
warm

Adverbs
at night
awfully
especially
fairly
more
much more
only
pretty
too
very
yet

Conjunction
so

Other words
enough
less . . . than
more . . . than
(not) as . . . as

Expressions
Hello?
All right.
OK.
Yeah, but sometimes . . .
That's outrageous!

How about . . . ?
That sounds interesting.

Let's compare . . . and . . .
Let's talk about . . .
What's . . . like?
It needs a little work.
What do you like most about it?

4 I've never heard of that!

Grammar

1. Countable and uncountable nouns

Countable singular	Countable plural	Uncountable
a bean	(some) beans	butter
a dish	(some) dishes	cheese
an egg	(some) eggs	chicken
a meal	(some) meals	cream
a mushroom	(some) mushrooms	flour
a recipe	(some) recipes	garlic
a sandwich	(some) sandwiches	ham
a snack	(some) snacks	homework
a spice	(some) spices	honey
a tomato	(some) tomatoes	jam
a vegetable	(some) vegetables	juice
		lamb
		meat
		milk
		oil
		paper
		pork
		tea

Words often used with uncountable nouns

a bag of sugar	**a package of** butter
a bottle of wine	**a piece of** cake
a bowl of soup	**a pound of** flour
a can of beer	**a slice of** bread
a carton of milk	**a tablespoon of** salt
a cup of oil	**a teaspoon of** sugar
a jar of jam	

2. For past tense of irregular verbs, see page 133.

Key Vocabulary

Nouns
appetizer
banana
barbecue
beverage
bowl
brains
bread
cabbage
cheesecake
chicken
class
dessert
fortune teller
frog
garlic
helicopter
homework
honey
ice cream
ingredient
leg
lemon
lighter fluid
milkshake
onion

peanut
peanut butter
piece
potato chip
restaurant
rollercoaster
sandwich
sauce
saucepan
sir
slice
snack
snail
soda
tablespoon
tomato juice
utensil
vegetable
weekend

Verbs
decide
drive
eat
eat out
fly

go skiing
learn how to
make
pour
put
sound
spread
type

Two-part verbs
chop up
clean up
cut up
get out
look up
pick up
pour on
pour over
put in
put on
take off
take out
turn on
turn over

Adjectives
awful
busy
delicious
fried
strange

Adverbs
ever
last
last time
last year
this year
today
yesterday

Prepositions
on top
over
with

Other words
anything
please
the other

Days of the week
Monday
Tuesday
Wednesday
Thursday
Friday
Saturday
Sunday

Expressions
Ugh!
I've never heard of that!
Like to try some?
I think I'll . . .
Can I look at yours?

5 Going places

Grammar

1. Modal verbs

Ability
I **can** speak Spanish.

Possibility
You **can** get traveler's checks at the bank.
You **could** buy a roundtrip ticket.
You **may** need a visa.
You **might** need a visa.

Suggestion
You **should**   take traveler's checks.
You **shouldn't** ...
You **ought to** ...
You **could**   ...
You**'d better** ...
I **would**   ...
I **wouldn't**   ...

Necessity
I **have to** get a visa.
I **don't have to** get a visa.
I **must** get a visa.

2. See page 133 for a list of tenses and verb forms.

3. Prepositions with time phrases

Seasons	Days of the week	Time
in the spring	on Monday	at 4 o'clock
in the summer	on Tuesday	until 4 o'clock
in the fall		
in the winter	**Events**	
	after class	
	before class	

4. For past tense of irregular verbs, see page 133.

Key Vocabulary

Nouns
advice
backpack
back pocket
camping gear
camping trip
cash
clothes
clothing
credit card
drink
father
friend
Halloween
health
health insurance
hitchhiking

hotel reservation
kind
luggage
medication
money
money belt
party
passport
place
plane ticket
roundtrip ticket
shorts
sleeping bag
Swiss Army knife
tent
thing
travel document

traveler's checks
trip
vaccination
visa
wallet
windbreaker

Verbs
bring
carry
check
going to
join
pack
plan
spend
stay

travel
want
wear

Adverbs
already
maybe

Modals
had better
have to
must
ought to
should
shouldn't
would

Wh-words and phrases
how long
how many
what kinds
what other
what should
what shouldn't
what things
what time
what would
which trip

Pronoun
yourself

Prepositions
around
until

Other words
a lot of
as
lots of
other
together
too many

Expressions
What do you think?
I've thought of that.
Would you like to ...?
Sure.

6 Sure! No problem!

Grammar

1. WILL/WON'T for intentions

I'll work late tonight.
I **won't** be late again.
I'll write you a check.

2. Direct and indirect objects

	Indirect object	Direct object
Lend	me	a dollar.
Give	her	a cup of coffee.
Give	them	their bags.
Get	her	something to eat.
Bring	us	something to drink.
Pass	me	the salt.
Write	him	a check.

Key Vocabulary

Nouns		Verbs	Two-part verbs	Adverbs	Expressions
afternoon	library	block	hang up	again	Excuse me.
bill	light	blow	keep down	completely	By the way, . . .
book	locker	bother	leave open	like	
car	machine	check	put away	on time	Oh, sure. I'd be glad to!
cassette player	mess	lend	put out	right away	OK. I'll do that.
cat	noise	mail	take back	right now	Sure! No problem!
chair	nonsmoking section	mind	turn down	still	
change	phone	move	turn off		I'm sorry. I can't right
check	radio	mow	turn up	**Prepositions**	now.
cigarette	record	owe		about	I'm sorry, but I'm busy.
coat	room	park	**Adjectives**	outside	I'm sorry.
cover	shoe	pass	due back		I'd rather not.
dollar	smoke	promise	late	**Other words**	
door	tennis racquet	realize	loud	I'll	What? You must be
driveway	tie	return	open	mine	kidding!
face	toy	smoke	overdue	some kind of	Gosh!
faucet	trash	wait	torn	someone	How come?
feet	TV		wrong		
lawn	VCR (videocassette				
letter	recorder)				
	yard				

7 What on earth is this?

Key Vocabulary

Nouns			weeds	plant	Adverbs	Expressions
air conditioner	glue	shampoo	wire	polish	now	What on earth is
battery	grass	soap		pull out	probably	this?
blender	knife	stamp	**Verbs**	repair		What's it for?
boots	lighter	stapler	break	run	**Other words**	
broom	lock	stationery	call	service	all	May I help you?
can	manager	street lamp	change	shorten	most	Let me have a look.
can opener	milk	suit	clap	spill	on the market	
cassette tape	motorcycle	tape	clean	stick	together	That's all!
CD player	nail	tea	clip	stop	twice	Thanks, anyway.
chopsticks	office supplies	television	cut	use		
cleaning supplies	paint	tie	drop			
cloth	pants	trash can	dryclean	**Adjectives**		
curtains	paper	tune	fix	funny		
detergent	paper clip	vacuum cleaner	hear	long		
envelope	pliers	VCR	keep	terrible		
fork	pocketknife	video	measure	terrific		
gadget	polish	wallpaper	mend	wonderful		
glasses	ruler	watch	peel			
	scissors	water				

8 Let's celebrate!

Grammar

1. Cardinal and ordinal numbers

Cardinal		Ordinal	
one	seven	first	seventh
two	eight	second	eighth
three	nine	third	ninth
four	ten	fourth	tenth
five	eleven	fifth	eleventh
six	twelve	sixth	twelfth

2. Determiners

All people . . .
Nearly all people . . .
Most . . .
A lot of . . .
Lots of . . .
Many . . .
Several . . .
Some . . .
A few . . .
Few . . .

3. Adverbs of frequency

People always
usually
often
sometimes
occasionally
hardly ever
never

Key Vocabulary

Nouns
activity
anniversary
announcement
bachelor party
birthday
bridal shower
bride
cake
card
celebration
ceremony
champagne
couple
dancing
festival

fireworks
flower
gift
groom
holiday
honeymoon
independence
kimono
month
newlyweds
occasion
parade
period
photo
present
reception

revolution
roast turkey
season
trick
wedding
worker

Months of the year
January
February
March
April
May
June
July

August
September
October
November
December

Verbs
celebrate
date
get engaged
get married
happen
hold
honor
invite
party

receive
remember
serve

Adjectives
beautiful
bridal
special

Colors
black
blue
brown
gray
green
orange

pink
purple
red
white
yellow
light green
dark green

Adverb
during

Wh-words
how old
what else
what kind
what type

Other words
a year or so
each other
most
something
their own

Expressions
Oh, I didn't know that.

---

9 Back to the future

Grammar

1. IF-clauses

With future reference
If it **rains**, we **won't go**.
If it **rains**, I **may/might stay** home.
If I **see** her, I **will tell** her.
If I **call** him, I **could give** him the message.

With imaginary situations
If I **found** some money, I **would/might take** it to the police.
If I **had** more time, I **would/might study** another language.

With imaginary situations in the past
If I **had found** some money, I **would/might have kept** it.

2. Adverbs for future time

Soon, people will . . .
Next year, . . .
In a few years, . . .
In the next few years, . . .
Within twenty years, . . .
In fifty years, . . .
In the future, . . .
In the next century, . . .
By 2050, . . .

Key Vocabulary

Nouns
cigarette butt
clean-up crew
computer
education
fine
future
grandma
ground
hour
jet
law
meat
moon
pack
park
past
pet
plane
planet
smoking
subway
supply
system

taxes
train
trash
world

Verbs
ban
bother
can't stand
chew
disgust
gain weight
get rid of
give up
hate
infuriate
pass
quit
raise
run out
rush around
save
travel
wish

Adjectives
angry
barking
disgusted
healthy
horrible
mad
ridiculous

Adverbs
ago
around
nowadays
probably
soon
these days

Conjunction
because

Prepositions
against
by

Other words
better off
less
more than
up to

Expressions
I couldn't live without . . .
I'm really hooked on . . .
The trouble is, though . . .
You know . . .
In some ways . . .
Like what?
Got a match?
Uh-huh.
I guess so.
Me, too.

10 I don't like working overtime

Grammar

Adverbs of degree

I can type **very** fast.
       pretty fast.
       fairly fast.

I can't type **very** fast.

I'm **very** good at languages.
pretty good at languages.
fairly good at languages.

I'm not **very** good at languages.

Key Vocabulary

Nouns
boss
certificate
commuting
diploma
driver's license
economics
experience
husband
lifeguard
manners
math
next-door neighbor
overtime
personal secretary
phone number
promise
report
sales manager
salesperson
sales work
skill
spelling
tour guide
word processor

Verbs
be good at
enjoy
laugh
meet
worry
write

Modal verbs
can
can't

Adjectives
bad
bad-tempered
creative
easygoing
fast
forgetful
friendly
generous
helpful
impatient
intelligent
patient
polite
prejudiced
regular
reliable
serious
shy
smart
sociable
talkative

Adverbs
deeply
pretty
well

Other words
neither . . .
so . . .
a nine-to-five job

Expressions
Sounds interesting.
So-so.
About average.
I guess so.
Not really.
Actually, no.

11 It's really worth seeing!

Grammar

1. Prepositions with time phrases

Years
in 1911
in the 1960s
during the eighties

Centuries
in the fifteenth century
during the 20th century

Events
before World War II
during the Vietnam War
after the French Revolution

2. Determiners

A lot of oil . . .
A great deal of . . .
Lots of . . .
A large amount of . . .
A considerable amount of . . .

Not much cotton . . .
Not very much . . .
Very little . . .
Hardly any . . .
No . . .

3. For past tense of irregular verbs, see page 133.

Key Vocabulary

Nouns
art gallery
bridge
canal
capital
church
cotton
currency
grade school
information
invention
kilometer
light bulb
memorial
monument
mural
museum
novel
observatory
phonograph
province
rice
rubber
shrine
song
statue
temple
territory
test
travel agent
tunnel
yen

Verbs
complete
compose
design
discover
drive
export
govern
grow
locate
make up
manufacture
paint
produce
quiz
teach

Adjectives
ancient
right

Adverb
widely

Other word
both

Expressions
Go ahead.
Oh, that's right.
I'm not sure.
I really have no idea.
How would I know?
Is English spoken much there?
Oh, sorry, wrong number.

12 It's been a long time!

Grammar

1. Adverbials of time

> for about six months
> for eighteen months
> for less than a year
> for the last two years
> for ages
> for a long time
> for as long as I can remember
> less than a year ago
> over a year ago
> since my childhood
> since I got married
> since then
> since that time
> this time last year
> the year before last

Key Vocabulary

Nouns
actress
comic book
cosmetics
course
date
diving competition
dormitory
drama
driver's test
graduation
grandparents
life
parents
part

relationship
star
studio
wife

Verbs
commute
divorce
get to
jog
separate
walk

Adjectives
broke
same
unusual

Adverbs
back
next door
over a year
right after
unfortunately

Preposition
since

Other words
a little more
all your life

Expressions
It's been a long time.
It didn't work out.
Is that so?
How interesting!
Oh, really?
How about you?

2. See page 133 for a list of tenses and verb forms.

13 A terrible book, but a terrific movie!

Grammar

Verbs with prepositions

> I am amazed **at/by** ...
> I was bored **by/with** ...
> He is excited **at/by** ...
>   fascinated **by/in** ...
>   interested **in** ...
>   pleased **at/with** ...
>   surprised **at/by** ...
>   worried **by** ...

Key Vocabulary

Nouns
actor
astronaut
character
comedy
composer
director
event
guy
horror movie
horror story
medieval
million
mission
music
musical
nature film
popcorn
reaction
science fiction
story
western

Verbs
come over
end
kill
rent
stand around
star
take place

Other verbs
be bored by/with
be fascinated by
be interested in
be surprised that/by

Adjectives
best
better
boring
crazy
disgusting

dreadful
dumb
excellent
fantastic
fascinating
fatal
macho
main
marvelous
odd
outstanding
pathetic
silly
stupid
successful
surprising
weird

Relative pronouns
that
which
who

Other words
all
not ... at all

Expressions
What's on?
What's it about?
How about ... ?
Why don't you ... ?
I can't stand ...
Oh, come on!
Not really.
Good idea!

14 Say what you mean!

Key Vocabulary

Nouns
appointment
argument
belly dancing
cloud
conversation
disagreement
excuse
falling rock
flu
hairdresser
handicapped
highway
hill
ice skating
idiom
invitation
lane
lesson
line
lining
masseur
parking space
pedestrian crossing

penny
plan
poison
proverb
reason
road
road construction
road sign
saying
silver
slang
stitch
traffic
U-turn
wheelchair
wrestling match

Verbs
apologize
approach
burn
cause
criticize
earn

feel
get around
promise
recall
translate
watch out
wonder

Modal verbs
can
could
may
might
must
should

Adjectives
arrogant
confident
confused
confusing
controversial
diligent

divorced
glad
hard-working
puzzled
reserved
slippery
steep
strong
sure
wet

Adverbs
ahead
anyway
perhaps
straight

Other words
another
every

Expression
We can see the sights.

15 What would you do?

Key Vocabulary

Nouns
aunt
beach
boat
burglar
casino
cigarette lighter
deodorant
drinking problem
error
exam
father-in-law
house guest
jewelry
lottery
luck
mistake
neighbor
note
owner
park bench
police
salesclerk
shoplifting
window
winning number

Verbs
accept
admit
agree
bet
borrow
break
cheat
choose
deny
disagree
discover
dislike
exchange
faint
fight
get rid of
guess
lie
lock
lose
point out
prefer
refuse
sail
smell
steal
swim
warn

Adjective
valuable

Adverbs
luckily
overseas

Other words
all at once
no one
piece of
someone
something else
though

Expressions
How come . . . ?
Thank goodness!
No way!

Irregular verbs

Present	Past	Participle	Present	Past	Participle
be: am/is, are	was, were	been	know	knew	known
bet	bet	bet	leave	left	left
blow	blew	blown	lend	lent	lent
break	broke	broken	lose	lost	lost
bring	brought	brought	make	made	made
build	built	built	mean	meant	meant
buy	bought	bought	meet	met	met
catch	caught	caught	mow	mowed	mown
choose	chose	chosen	put	put	put
come	came	come	quit	quit	quit
cost	cost	cost	run	ran	run
cut	cut	cut	say	said	said
do	did	done	see	saw	seen
drive	drove	driven	sell	sold	sold
eat	ate	eaten	send	sent	sent
feel	felt	felt	show	showed	shown
fight	fought	fought	sit	sat	sat
find	found	found	speak	spoke	spoken
fly	flew	flown	spend	spent	spent
forget	forgot	forgotten	spread	spread	spread
get	got	gotten	stand	stood	stood
give	gave	given	steal	stole	stolen
go	went	gone	stick	stuck	stuck
grow	grew	grown	swim	swam	swum
hang	hung/hanged	hung/hanged	take	took	taken
have	had	had	tell	told	told
hear	heard	heard	wear	wore	worn
hide	hid	hidden	win	won	won
hold	held	held	write	wrote	written
keep	kept	kept			

Tenses and verb forms

Present and past tenses

Simple present	I **live** in New York.
Present continuous	I **am living** in New York.
Present perfect	I **have lived** in New York for two years.
Present perfect continuous	I **have been living** in New York for two years.
Simple past	I **lived** in New York two years ago.
Past continuous	I **was living** in New York two years ago.
Past perfect	I **had worked** there for two years.
Past perfect continuous	I **had been working** there for two years.

Describing the future

With simple present	I **leave** tomorrow.
With present continuous	I **am leaving** tomorrow.
With **going to**	I **am going to leave** tomorrow.
With **will**	I **will leave** tomorrow.

Comparative and superlative adjectives (continues on page 134)

1. Adjectives with -ER and -EST (e.g., angry, angri**er,** and angri**est**)

angry	cheap	cool	dumb	funny	hot	long	mad	odd	shy	smart	strong	wet
big	clean	crazy	fast	great	large	loud	near	old	silly	steep	warm	
busy	cold	dirty	friendly	healthy	late	lovely	nice	safe	small	strange	weird	

2. Adjectives with MORE and MOST (e.g., arrogant, **more** arrogant, **most** arrogant)

arrogant	confusing	easygoing	impatient	prejudiced	stupid
awful	controversial	exciting	intelligent	reasonable	successful
bad-tempered	creative	expensive	interesting	regular	surprising
beautiful	crowded	fascinating	modern	reliable	talkative
boring	dangerous	forgetful	pathetic	ridiculous	terrible
comfortable	delicious	generous	patient	serious	terrific
commercial	diligent	hard-working	pleasant	slippery	valuable
confident	disgusting	helpful	polite	sociable	wonderful
confused	dreadful	horrible	polluted	special	

3. Irregular adjectives

good	better	best
bad	worse	worst

Answer to Unit 1, Exercise 6

Julio Iglesias

Answers to Unit 11, Exercise 10.1

a) in North Africa
b) French and Flemish
c) Indonesia and Malaysia
d) Burma, Hong Kong, India, Kenya, Malaysia, Nigeria, Pakistan, the Philippines, Singapore, Sri Lanka, Sudan, Tanzania, among other countries
e) Belgium, Canada, France, Haiti, Luxembourg, Morocco, Senegal, Switzerland, Tunisia, among other countries
f) Australia, Canada, Denmark, Italy, Great Britain, Japan, Malaysia, the Netherlands, Norway, Portugal, Spain, Sweden, among other countries

Answers to Interchange 13

a) *Jaws*
b) *Family Business, Rain Man, Tootsie, Kramer versus Kramer, The Graduate*, and *Midnight Cowboy*, among others
c) Paul Newman
d) Bette Midler, Liza Minnelli, Dolly Parton, Barbra Streisand, Willie Nelson, and Frank Sinatra, among others
e) *The Birds, Dial M for Murder, North by Northwest, Notorious, Psycho, Rear Window, Strangers on a Train*, and *Suspicion*, among others
f) Bela Lugosi played Dracula; Boris Karloff played Frankenstein.
g) Sean Connery, Roger Moore, Timothy Dalton
h) Ingrid Bergman
i) *Harlem Nights, Coming to America, Beverly Hills Cop I* and *II, 48 Hours, Another 48 Hours,* among others
j) *King Kong*